TOUCHING THE EDGE

A MOTHER'S SPIRITUAL PATH FROM LOSS TO LIFE

Margaret Wurtele

For Martha and Bruce
With love,

Margaret 3·14·03

WILEY

John Wiley & Sons, Inc.

Published by John Wiley & Sons, Inc., Hoboken, New Jersey
Published simultaneously in Canada

Design and production by Navta Associates, Inc.

For general information about our other products and services, please contact our Customer Care Department within the United States at (800) 762-2974, outside the United States at (317) 572-3993 or fax (317) 572-4002.

Wiley also publishes its books in a variety of electronic formats. Some content that appears in print may not be available in electronic books.

Library of Congress Cataloging-in-Publication Data:
Wurtele, Margaret.
      Touching the edge : a mother's spiritual path from loss to life / Margaret Wurtele.
            p. cm.
Includes bibliographical references and index.
      ISBN 0-471-22287-9
      1. Bereavement–Psychological aspects. 2. Grief. 3. Teenagers–Death–Psychological aspects. 4. Loss (Psychology) I. Title.
      BF575.G7 .W87 2003
      155.9'37––dc21   2002014023

Printed in the United States of America

10 9 8 7 6 5 4 3 2 1

The author gratefully acknowledges the following for permission to quote from:

The Poems of Emily Dickinson, Thomas H. Johnson, ed., Cambridge, Mass.: The Belknap Press of Harvard University Press, Copyright © 1951, 1955, 1979 by the President and Fellows of Harvard College.

"Dirge Without Music" by Edna St. Vincent Millay. Copyright © 1928, 1955 by Edna St. Vincent Millay and Norma Millay Ellis. All rights reserved. Reprinted by permission of Elizabeth Barnett, literary executor.

A Door in the Hive by Denise Levertov, copyright © 1989 by Denise Levertov. Reprinted by permission of New Directions Publishing Corp.

Breathing the Water by Denise Levertov, copyright © 1987 by Denise Levertov. Reprinted by permission of New Directions Publishing Corp.

Dream Work by Mary Oliver, copyright © 1986 by Mary Oliver. Used by permission of Grove/Atlantic, Inc.

"If each day falls ..." by Pablo Neruda, translated by William O'Daly, from *The Sea and the Bells*. Copyright © 1973 by Pablo Neruda and Heirs of Pablo Neruda. English translation copyright © 1988, 2002 by William O'Daly. Reprinted with the permission of Copper Canyon Press, P.O. Box 271, Port Townsend, WA 96368.

"Little Gidding" in *Four Quartets*, copyright 1942 by T.S. Eliot and renewed 1970 by Esme Valerie Eliot, reprinted by permission of Harcourt, Inc.

The Poems of J.V. Cunningham. Reprinted with permission of Swallow Press/Ohio University Press, Athens, Ohio.

The Gold Cell by Sharon Olds, copyright © 1987 by Sharon Olds. Used by permission of Alfred A. Knopf, a division of Random House, Inc. "Cambridge Elegy" first appeared in *POETRY*, copyright © October 1981 by The Modern Poetry Association, and is reprinted by permission of the Editor of *POETRY*.

True Companion, Words and Music by Marc Cohn. Copyright © 1991 by Famous Music Corporation. International Copyright Secured. All Rights Reserved.

The Selected Poems of Wendell Berry, copyright © Wendell Berry. Used by permission of the publisher.

The Essential Rumi, copyright © 1995 by Coleman Barks, translator.

For Chris, Andrew, and Heidi,
with love

CONTENTS

Acknowledgments

The writing of this book has been a long and valuable exercise. First, I want to thank my husband, Angus, who has supported me every day of our marriage; who patiently allowed me the time and space to write; who faithfully read each page, each chapter, many times. To my mother and father, I send appreciation for taking the time to read, to listen, and to respond and for opening themselves again and again to the pain of grief in so doing. To the members of my family and to my friends who read the manuscript and encouraged me, thank you.

I am grateful to Paulette Bates Alden for providing me with a writing group whose members' honest feedback was critical to the inception and early drafts of this project. Paulette was an enthusiastic reader and first editor. Without her support, I might not have taken the plunge.

I am indebted to Mike Gauthier and to Bruce Barcott, author of *The Measure of a Mountain*, for their accounts of the accident on

Mount Rainier and its aftermath. I have relied on Mike's memory and Bruce's reporting in that book for the story I recreated here.

Gail See—as always—has been a cheerleader and advocate of immeasurable value. Without her, the book might never have seen the light of day. I want to thank my agent, Jonathon Lazear, and Christi Cardenas at the Lazear Agency for believing in this book and patiently persevering until it found a home.

My editor, Tom Miller, has been an empathetic partner. He acquired the manuscript from his heart, and he has improved it with talent and critical skill. Tom has been truly engaged—thoughtful, thorough, and enthusiastic—the kind of editor I didn't know existed anymore.

And Phil—you have been and will always be my inspiration and my guide.

Prologue

One hot August night in 1995, as I slept soundly in Minneapolis, exhausted from a day filled with weekend houseguests, my twenty-two-year-old son Philip Otis set off on a mission in Mount Rainier Park. He and Sean Ryan, a young climbing ranger, had been sent to help rescue a man with a broken ankle, stranded somewhere just below the mountain's summit. As they climbed that night, the weather turned fierce. They had been having equipment problems, and at 11:30 P.M. radio contact was lost. At some point, they fell, roped together, tumbling over the icy slopes to their deaths twelve hundred feet below.

I dreamed peacefully that night as my worst nightmare was unfolding half a continent away. I didn't hear the news of Phil's death until almost two days later, a lightning bolt that cleaved my life in two. He was my only biological child, much of what I had been living for.

I was about to turn fifty, absorbed in an intense midlife spiritual awakening. Suddenly I felt utterly betrayed by a God I had only just embraced. Now, I thought, my life was over, and as a massive fog of pain and grief moved in, I could see no way out.

In the months that followed, I experienced an outpouring of love. I was carried along as if borne up on the hands and shoulders of my family and friends. I floated on a wave of letters, small gifts, thoughts, and prayers that refused to let me touch the ground.

One day, in the weeks after Phil's death, I was riding in an open convertible, one of his journals on the seat beside me. The wind flipped the cover open, ruffling the pages, and in a flash—just as I used to reach an arm instinctively in front of my child on a fast brake—I held the book down for dear life. *Is this it?* I wondered. Is this all that is left: a few photographs that will surely fade, some letters and books of his writing that will turn to dust, the memories cherished by his family and friends, who—like him—will die too?

A year or so later, as I began to consider writing this book, crushing doubts enveloped me. How could I examine a life so intimately entwined with mine and achieve any distance, any perspective? When I searched, at first all I could find were broken bits of memory that came briefly into focus, then dissolved. I felt as if I were wandering the dusty plateau of an ancient Israeli *tel*, a site of holy ruins. I would pick up a fragment, turn it in my hand, and try to let it be a clue to reveal a wider history, a greater story.

One May evening that first year, I was attending my college reunion in Massachusetts and dinner was winding down. I gazed at one of my classmates, decades older but still oddly the same as when we graduated from this women's college thirty years before. Why were we there? I searched her eyes for some explanation of our decision to come a thousand miles to our reunion, to sleep in bare dorm rooms and drink bad coffee. "I come for the stories," she said. Yes, and so had

I. My own story of loss had been told again and again that day, held out like an open hand, an invitation. I had been offered their stories in return—stories that resonated with mine, expanded me, and revealed them.

Salman Rushdie wrote, "Those who do not have power over the story that dominates their lives, power to retell it, to rethink it, deconstruct it, joke about it, and change it as times change, truly are powerless." So I am seeking power of a sort, the power to reclaim my own life in the wake of this death, the power to tell Phil's story, the power to fill the void. I want to gather the waves and particles of his energy, spin a three-dimensional holographic image where the beams of recollection intersect in space, merge them back together into a living, shimmering whole.

Phil's story is of a life lived with gusto, an ordinary kid whose dreams and destiny led him to the edge. I hope his story will inspire others like him to trust themselves and to risk failure in pursuit of who they really are. My story is of a mother's journey, of love and loss and the rebirth of spirit, that I hope will encourage other parents to trust destiny's mysterious call in their children's lives and to learn to let go in spite of their fears. For those who, like me, have had to cope with unspeakable loss, I hope my words can bring a measure of comfort and help chart a path toward new life.

CHAPTER 1

Questions of Spirit

What is necessary, after all, is only this: solitude, vast, inner solitude. To walk inside yourself and meet no one for hours.

Rainer Maria Rilke

It was the summer of 1986, the first one in years that actually felt like summer. I had quit a full-time job earlier that year to spend more time with my son Phil, who had just turned thirteen. He seemed hardly to notice my presence, so absorbed was he in his friends and sports. To my surprise, it was I who felt utterly new.

I was relaxed, far less busy, and I was preoccupied, becoming aware of a new consciousness that had swelled into the pockets of stillness my days now offered. I woke early most mornings, when the light was easing up over the marsh and birds called from the branches of the trees just outside our bedroom windows. I would set off, up the driveway, the crunch of my shoes on the gravel interrupting the natural sounds of morning. I might break a strand of a spider's trail across my forehead, sidestep a hapless frog flattened by a late-night car. I might notice a dandelion gone to seed or a sumac pod swollen where a blossom used to be. On those walks I felt transparent, like a traveling lens that could take the world in as it came, accurately, freely, unshaped by judgment or projection. This circuit became a kind of mantra for me, as I passed each familiar house, each bend in the road, each bit of landscape. I depended on them to set the pace for the day, to orient me in a way to a new openness.

I had taken up yoga again too. Thirteen years before, as a new mother, I had discovered the ancient discipline, taking Saturday classes, practicing faithfully for a year or so. But the demands of a new baby and the pressures of what became single motherhood had intervened, making it impossible to continue. The previous year I had tried again. I found a teacher I loved, a class near my house, and—with the new time that unemployment gave me—I had become a dedicated student again.

I loved yoga class. I worked so hard, stretching and aligning my body. The intricacies of each pose—the position of my feet, thighs, hips, spine, and shoulders—demanded a kind of focused attention that I had not experienced. Yoga was unlike attention at work or at play, attention that drew me out to the world. This awareness drew me strongly into myself and beyond, to a suspended mental state in which thoughts and fantasies, worries and anxiety were crowded out and irrelevant, where the only thing that mattered was utter awareness of the orientation of limbs, muscle, sinew, even blood flow, all in an attempt to hold myself in a harmonious, graceful posture.

At the end of class, exhausted from the effort, we were invited to lie on the floor in *savasana*, the "corpse" pose. Limbs outstretched, we relaxed every quivering muscle one by one, starting from the scalp and moving, inch by inch, down to the soles of our feet. Again, all my attention was fixed on this journey, unwavering, focused. The utter calm, the peace, the isolation from everything else became for me a kind of prayer.

"Prayer" had always felt wrong to me. In our family growing up, the concept had been like watching soap operas on television or engaging in ethnic slurs. Prayer just wasn't done. My bright young parents were eagerly ethical; they believed in reading and in the life of the mind. They were active and outdoorsy, but religion—or anything that smacked of "spirituality"—was considered outside the bounds of worthy pursuit. It wasn't bad; it just wasn't for them, for us. I understood that religion—and particularly the Christianity of our forebears—was speculative at best, and therefore perhaps even a little frivolous. I gleaned that its followers were unquestioning, needy, perhaps too easily led. In my parents' lively agnosticism, "God" was an anthropomorphic label that oversimplified science and nature, that substituted a supernatural shoulder to cry on when earnest psychology and in-depth personal exploration would result in more mature growth.

I knew about prayer, of course. Grace was said before dinner at my friend Ann's house, and I—like every child—had somehow picked up NowIlaymedowntosleep. . . . But I had been given no framework for it. Praying seemed just odd to me, like living by the ocean or speaking a foreign language. I assumed I was expected to agree with my parents. The first child and eager to please, I was timid and ashamed of the huge questions that floated around the edges of my consciousness, the yearnings in which I secretly indulged.

One of my best friends in grade school was Catholic. I stared, already fascinated with the crucifix that hung above her bed, at the palm frond she stuck into it just before Easter and left there to turn stiff and yellow for months afterward. I tagged along with her family occasionally to Sunday mass and ate it up. I didn't necessarily believe in anything; I just wanted some recognition of mystery in my life.

Our family joined the Unitarian Society for several years in answer to my pleas. We had Sunday "forums" and "celebrations" of various natural seasons, but where was God? Where was Jesus? Why wasn't it called "church" so I could say I went to one? I might as well have been at school or summer camp. I was as embarrassed by this new affiliation as I had been by our stay-at-home Sundays.

As I grew, I took on my parents' attitudes. I absorbed the liturgy of humanism and natural science. Instead of hymns, I memorized the lyrics to Urban League records. The catechism of doubt took hold, turning me into a confirmed agnostic, one who was polite and tolerant but who felt intellectually superior to any version of a believer.

Now here I was that summer of 1986, the mother of a thirteen-year-old-boy, Phil, my only child. I had recently passed forty, and new life was stirring in me, life of a spiritual nature. Despite the intensity of the yoga—or perhaps because of it—I could no longer see myself as just a body with a thinking motor, one that was born of a human animal mother and would just tick away like a windup clock until I stopped altogether at the hour of my death. I felt bigger than my body, bigger than my brain. I was becoming expanded somehow, opened up. Maybe it was a midlife crisis, but surely the landscape had shifted. A new path beckoned to me, and I was eager to see where it would lead.

Later that summer, I was sitting in the office of the Episcopal bishop of Minnesota. I had come in desperation, because I needed help, and he was the only member of the clergy I knew personally. I had met him about ten years earlier, when Phil and I were en route to visit my grandmother in Tucson. Our plane was delayed for an hour or so in Denver, and the bishop and I had struck up a conversation. He had impressed me then with his warmth and openness, and so I had called him, hoping he would remember me.

I felt as if he was towering over me, but he was wearing an open-collared blue shirt, not the purple one with the stiff white collar I had expected. So I took heart. I told him about all the books I had been reading obsessively, about the yoga and how I was drawn to Eastern religions. He seemed to be listening carefully. I took a deep breath.

"Actually, I think I want to explore Christianity, but I don't think it will ever be possible for me."

"Why not?" He was listening, interested.

"Because I could never recite the creed," I said. "I don't think I could ever believe what it says."

I waited, sure he would send me packing. But he looked intently at me. He didn't seem shocked or even surprised. He stood up and began pacing around the office, pausing first near the bookshelves, then in front of the colorful yellow oil painting that dominated one wall.

"Why don't you try thinking of it as a song?" he said. He turned his back to me and began reciting the Nicene Creed gently, rhythmically. He didn't linger over each word, but he let it flow, creating an atmosphere, a kind of invitation.

Something cracked inside of me. I felt a little explosion, like a blast opening the entrance to a tunnel. I heard him refer to the creed as "poetry." I heard him giving me permission to think of it that way—like art or music.

After that day, I felt I had made a choice. I was sure I wanted to see if Christianity would work for me. I continued to take yoga, to explore meditation, and to read freely in Eastern as well as Christian literature. But in my daily life, in my heart, I started down the Christian path in earnest.

I began to go to church nearly every Sunday. My husband Angus was a cradle Episcopalian, and he was eager to take up where he had left off years before when he had let it all go. We went together to St. Mark's Cathedral in downtown Minneapolis. The gothic spaces soared; the music was sublime. I felt a little like an imposter, like a guest crashing the party, but I took the *Book of Common Prayer* in hand and I recited the creed when the time came. Part of me still clenched up when I read, "born of the Virgin Mary" or "seated at the right hand of the Father," but the other part of me said *It's OK! It's poetry!* So I kept reading.

I began to see two ways to think: with my head and with my heart. If I stayed in my head, I brought tests to bear on the text: measures of history and science, questions of feasibility or verifiability. But if I stayed in my heart, I looked not for true statements but for truth, not for fact but for feeling.

I listened to Scripture the same way. I took in the stories, but I set them free inside of me. I played with them. I considered the dynamics of the characters, put myself in the settings. I began to see that the Bible and Christian liturgy were tools. Rather than things that I was being asked to "believe" against my better judgment, they were rich storehouses of wisdom, poetic images and metaphors passed down through time, that I could dip into at will and apply to my own life.

Like the story of Abraham and Sarah. I resonated with this tale about the woman who was old, who had lived for years trying to have a child and who had nearly given up. That experience had almost been mine with Phil.

CHAPTER 2

The View from the Bottom

By your favor, O LORD, you had established me as a
strong mountain.

NRSV Psalm 30:7

I had always assumed that I would have children, just as my parents
had had me. I had met Todd, Phil's father and my first husband, in
high school, on a bus trip the summer before our senior year. We had
both been elected president of the student council at our respective
single-sex schools. We had joined a bus full of other officers from
around the state of Minnesota to travel to a student council convention in Anaheim. Disneyland was to be part of the action. I saw Todd
sitting alone at the back of the bus, reading (*Catcher in the Rye*, I
think). What snared me was the obvious courage it took for him to sit
back there while the rest of us were chatting and getting to know each
other. He and I sat together every day after that, watching the cornfields give way to prairie, then mountains, and we told each other the
stories of our lives. We laughed a lot. A five-year veteran of a
girls' school, a sister with no brothers, I had never had a male friend
before. Like me, Todd was a Democrat in a Republican school, and
best of all—he had grown up in a family of Unitarians as agnostic

and secular as mine. By the time the bus rolled into the parking lot in Minneapolis a couple of weeks later, we were in love. I couldn't imagine spending my life with anyone else.

I was born in November 1945, just after VJ Day, on the cutting edge of the baby boom. I was a child of the fifties, when America was victorious, strong, and confidently building its future. Patriotism, pride, and faith in democracy were at the heart of what we believed, of who we were. I walked down the aisle at my high school commencement conscious that our country was in the hands of a young, brilliant new president. I knew I would join the Peace Corps, because it was one of the things I could "do for my country."

Six months later, Kennedy was shot. The war in Vietnam followed. My male friends, whose fathers had once eagerly enlisted, exhausted their ingenuity seeking ways to avoid the draft. I traveled to Washington to protest a bombing, and—along with most of my college classmates—I strapped a black armband over the sleeve of my commencement robe to register disappointment that the graduation speaker was a member of Nixon's cabinet.

We both went east to college, where we dated for four years, traveling nearly every weekend the two hours of highway that separated us. We married in my parents' garden a couple of weeks after my graduation. He had to miss his own commencement so that we could squeeze the wedding in before Peace Corps training started. After two years in West Africa and a year in New York City, we returned to Minneapolis to work.

At first we were ambivalent about having children, not wanting to end the life the two of us had enjoyed as a couple. Nonetheless, we began trying to conceive. At first, we went about it casually, but when nothing happened after months of mild intention, we began to try in earnest. We worked first on our timing, then moved on to thermometers and pills, enduring month after month of disappointment and heartbreak. I was only twenty-six, but like Sarah, I felt old. I was in despair, convinced I would never conceive, never have a child, never be the mother I dreamed of being. Then, three years into the process, I missed a period.

I remember that October day in 1972, sitting in my obstetrician's office. I had dressed hurriedly and nervously after the exam. This time I was sure I was pregnant, but it had yet to be confirmed. He knocked, then entered smiling. "What are you doing Memorial Day weekend?" he asked. My heart leaped.

Todd and I rejoiced later that day. We called the new grandparents together, saying we wanted them to meet a mystery guest. Before dinner, we popped open a bottle of champagne and toasted this new being who waited in the dark to be born.

In May 1973, a wedding and the Peace Corps behind me, I lay on a couch in the hospital maternity lounge in labor, watching the Watergate hearings. This was disillusion heaped on disappointment. With every breath and with every push that I mustered to bring my contribution to the next generation into the world, the values that had shaped my own were being shredded before me. At least, I thought, we'll still have family: this new son and the life the three of us would have together.

From the beginning, it seemed, Phil's life was about mountains. At first, he simply *was* one. From the moment he was born, Phil was substantial, solid. Some babies I knew were wiry and delicate, but nothing was precarious about mine. As he grew, he took on a Buddha-like aspect. He was loath to move and expected that the world would come to him. He was right. A first child, first grandchild, first nephew, he was surrounded by an eager, doting family who sought to satisfy his every desire. Food was paramount. He nursed voraciously, then took to cereal and applesauce with a vengeance. He ate, then sat, then ate some more. His limbs began to lose their definition, puffing into a series of soft pillows with creases where the joints should have been. His neck and chin began to merge, and the broad sunny smile that was his bait and snare had to move avalanches of flesh in order to spread across his face. Because he didn't move, he learned to talk, to announce in a sure voice what he wanted: a book to be read to him, a particular toy, the next meal. I was frantic. Why didn't he roll over or try to rise up on hands and knees? My friends' babies were constantly underfoot, crawling, hauling themselves up on the furniture. Mine watched, amused, but he was in no hurry to join the fray. He didn't walk until he was two.

Todd and I had been married, I began to understand, much too soon. We had dated for five years, and we had both wanted to join the Peace Corps. Postponing marriage was not an option. We had wanted to have sex, guilt-free, and marriage was the only way to get it. When I finally had Phil, I thought we had everything, that our marriage had settled into its now-familiar patterns and would play out as I had always assumed it would: summers by a northern lake, Christmases around a fire, more children, friends, dogs, and satisfying careers. But that was my side of the story.

To my husband, such a prospect was confining, even frightening. Married at twenty-one, he had never played the field or lived alone. He was quiet and reticent. What I took to be tacit endorsement of my articulated dreams and myriad household decisions had instead been resentment, even rage, summarily swallowed. One day, when Phil was several months old, after a couple of weeks of coming home late for dinner and walking around in a fog of growing remoteness, my husband announced he didn't love me anymore. He wanted out.

We tried months of counseling to no avail. After several false starts, tearful reunions, and angry recriminations, on a spring day shortly after Phil's first birthday, he walked out the door for good. I felt the floor tilt as the walls of my psyche realigned themselves. All of my assumptions had been rendered obsolete. I looked at my baby, sitting placidly and innocently on the floor.

The view from the bottom was straight up. Anger weighed me down like a heavy pack—anger at Todd for leaving me, anger at myself for failing to please him, for failing Phil, for driving his father away. There was sadness too. I grieved for the man I loved and for the future I had counted on for me and my son. I was afraid too, as I contemplated the risks ahead. I tortured myself with visions of lonely nights. I worried about finding a job, wondered how I would support the two of us. I dreaded the pity I imagined I would experience from my friends. I despaired of ever finding anyone else to love. I couldn't eat; I couldn't sleep. My whole world went black. As if I had been roped to my husband for survival and now he had cut the cord, I felt helpless, alone, and terrified.

Phil learned to crawl, then to walk. He never looked back. The early months of immobility simply disappeared, their stored energy exploding into a life of action. The extra layers of fat melted away, the limbs were leaner and strong now, but we still cuddled up after dinner together to read before bed.

One night, when Phil was three, a visitor joined us in the ritual. Angus and I had been seeing each other steadily for a month or so. Our first date had been a business meeting. As the development officer of St. Paul's united arts fund, I was searching desperately for corporate dollars to help achieve a challenging goal. Angus was the young CEO of a thriving paint and coatings manufacturing company. I had known him slightly for years, ever since I had worked in membership and public relations for Walker Art Center and he was a member of the board. My parents were neighbors and friends of the Wurteles. A few months before, I had learned that Angus and his wife were separated, but it did not spark any particular interest. I was dating someone else at the time, a man active in politics, who had just left town to play a major role in the 1976 presidential campaign.

Angus stopped by the office to pick me up for lunch, and I

remember being struck by the energy that radiated from his small, neat body, the lively look in his eye. Over a sandwich at the local business club, I presented a sound case for a gift to the united arts fund. I knew my material well, and I delivered it with enthusiasm. He listened carefully, but then the conversation turned to more personal matters.

We discovered we had been traveling a common path. He, like me, had a spouse who had abruptly lost interest in him, whose desire for independence had made their marriage seem to her little more than a trap. He, like me, had been mystified, had desperately tried to convince her to stay. Like me, he had assumed they would be together for a lifetime. He told me, though he had suffered a great deal in recent months, that he was learning to be open about it to other people, discovering that his new vulnerability was less a barrier than an opportunity for connection. I listened; I resonated with all that he had to say. That he already had three children and was eleven years older gave me pause, but I was attracted to him. My current friend had been gone for weeks with no end in sight, so when Angus called a week or so later to invite me out to dinner, I said yes.

As we grew to know each other in the next few weeks, we found even more common ground. We had both grown up in Minneapolis, had graduated—years apart—from the same independent school. We had both gone east to college, then lived overseas, he in the Philippines with the navy, I in West Africa with the Peace Corps. We both loved tennis, classical music and contemporary art. We were both politically liberal. We had a lot of common friends and parallel sets of values and priorities.

More important, though, we were similar personality types. We were both high-energy, organized, and assertive. In my marriage to Todd, I had been told I was too dominant, that I made too many decisions, forced things to go my way; with Angus I had met my match. He beat me to the punch time after time. He had plans of his own to supersede mine, strong opinions that led me to back off more often than not. If I was eager, active, and in charge, he was more so. I loved it.

That night, as I was reading Phil his bedtime story, Angus sat on the other side of him on the living room couch. When I closed the cover of the book, Angus reached over and gently put a thumb and forefinger on either side of Phil's lumpy, three-year-old, dimpled knee. "That's a pretty nice knee," he said. "Do you like to have it tickled?"

Phil started to giggle. "No . . . ," he said, grinning, with an ever-so-slight lift in his voice: a definite invitation.

Angus applied a slight pressure with his fingers on either side of the knee. Phil dissolved in a paroxysm of giggles, wrenching away, rolling on the floor. He stood up and threw himself at Angus, hugging his knees, laughing. Then he shouted, "You can't tickle me!" and ran to the other side of the room. It was then, I think, that I decided to marry Angus, even though I hadn't been asked.

That April, seven months after we began seeing each other, I received a call. "There's a house I want you to look at," he said. It was three blocks from the gray Cape Cod that Phil and I lived in, right on the lake we loved to walk around. Five blocks in the other direction, Angus's three kids—Chris, thirteen; Andrew, eleven; and Heidi, nine—were living with their mother.

"But I'm just leaving for a tennis game," I protested.

"I think you'd better come right now," he replied. "It's going to go on the open market tomorrow morning."

That night we sat together, scribbling on pieces of paper. We considered the asking price, how much I could get for my house, whether or not we should try to get the curtains and appliances included. One piece was missing. I looked up from the scribbles, searched his face. He looked at me and smiled. "We could move in in June," he said, "and get married in August." He hadn't proposed exactly, but he could read the yes in the smile that met his.

CHAPTER 3

Mountain Story

The truer you are to your daimon, the closer you are to
the death that belongs to your destiny.

James Hillman

In *The Soul's Code*, James Hillman recalls for us Plato's myth of Ur at
the end of *The Republic*. Before we are born, according to the myth, we
gather with all the individual souls together in the presence of three
Fates robed in white, turning the Spindle of Necessity, spinning to the
music of Sirens. We survey a vast array of lives of every description
and, assisted by a special "daimon" who has been assigned to guide us,
we choose a pattern to be lived out on earth. Within the path we
select, we will live with free choice, making us responsible for our
lives, but now we choose the time, the place, the very parents we need
to facilitate the living out of the story that has been sketched for us
like a cosmic road map. That story will be our acorn, the seed that
suggests the directions in which the tree of our life will grow. Then
we forget. We forget that we ever made a choice. We come into the
world a blank slate, and the deliberation is lost forever.

As the years of his childhood ticked away, Phil began to manifest
what seemed to be his own mountain story. He no longer resembled

a mountain himself; now he began to long for them. On a trip south to visit my grandmother in the Tucson desert, Phil—at seven—turned to me. "I want to come here to college," he announced.

I asked him why.

"Because of the mountains," he said, sweeping his arm around the view that surrounded us on every side with rugged peaks. "I have to live near the mountains."

He was drawn to heights—and the rush of a jump—from the time he was very small. These feelings were utterly foreign to me. As an adolescent, I spent one whole summer working up the nerve to dive off the high board at the local pool. Every August, I reluctantly climbed onto the Ferris wheel at the state fair, whooping as my stomach dropped out on the downward plunge. This "rush" was something I dreaded, not sought. For me the sensuous, all-consuming thrill was not worth the price I had to pay in fear. Phil was different. I marveled how someone with any of my genes could crave that gut-wrenching high. I watched his antics with admiration and anxiety.

One day, when he was not yet ten, I heard shouts from the back-yard. I poked my head out the door just in time to see Phil fly through the air, executing a long jump from the top of a wall by our garage across a twenty-foot-deep chasm to the roof of the screen porch six feet away. Then, to my horror, I heard him egging on a reluctant friend, urging him to follow in his wake. "Absolutely not!" I screamed just in time.

Several summers in a row in junior high, Phil traveled with a group of buddies to a cabin on the north shore of Lake Superior. The outings produced souvenir snapshots that took my breath away: sil-houettes of Phil and his friends, airborne, en route from a fifty-foot cliff down to the frigid waters of the lake below. "Do you check first to make sure it's deep enough?" I would ask, my heart leaping in my throat.

As Phil grew older, climbing became another outlet for his thrill seeking. The rappel down a vertical cliff, the suspense of being roped up, crossing an icy crevasse, the utter euphoria of reaching a summit fed his appetite in a responsible way. Phil was a good climber, a careful one. He received positive reports from the guides on his summer trips. He was a natural leader. He worked hard and was helpful to people who did not have as easy a time as he did. He kept up group morale with his infectious sense of humor. He wanted to be a guide some day.

One summer day when Phil was nearly out of high school, I passed him and a friend watching a videotape on television. I could hear a loud banshee yell on the soundtrack of a sequence they kept playing over and over. I stopped to take a look. The video was a promotional piece from Adrenaline Adventures, a bungee-jumping outfit in Boulder, Colorado. The tape showed twenty minutes or so of footage of clients, rubber tubing strapped to their ankles or harnessed to their stomachs, swan diving off railroad bridges or from a tethered hot-air balloon. Just before they hit the ground or the water, the tubing would reach its maximum stretch. They would bounce, inches from certain destruction. In between these shots, messages flashed on the screen: "A ship in the harbor is safe. But that's not what ships are built for"; or "Your body manufactures the most powerful drug known to man. . . . Experience it!" The last few seconds of the tape—the part they kept playing over and over—was a custom addition. The video showed Phil being strapped to a length of rubber tubing, climbing into the basket of a hot-air balloon, then rising seventy-five feet or so into the air. Phil stood up. The voices on the tape counted down: "Five, four, three, two, one." Without hesitation, he spread his arms and dove head first out of the balloon. "Yahoo!!" he shouted, when the strap caught. He bounced up and down in the air, fortunately quite far above the ground. He had actually paid for this privilege, using sixty dollars of his hard-earned money. I was speechless.

There was another leitmotif in Phil's emerging mountain story that kept pace with the urge to climb: a nascent impulse to respond to a call for rescue.

At six, Phil slept in Superman pajamas and often wore them well into the day. I made him a red cape, which he wore with panache over everything. "Can Superman really leap tall buildings in a single bound?" he asked. I hastened to assure him that a story is a story, afraid he might put the cape to the test.

In high school, Phil won a prize for his senior speech, entitled "Heroes." In it, he looked back on those childhood fantasies of heroic figures he had wished to emulate—figures of both light and darkness. Interspersed with fantasies of the outlaw Jesse James and Evel Knievel in all their dark feats of terror were memories of heroic episodes as Superman or Batman. "As human beings," Phil said in his speech, "we are given the gift of imagination, the ability to imagine ourselves as someone we admire, whether it be Martin Luther King, Mother Teresa, Han Solo, or Wonderwoman. Having these heroes in our lives helps us to grasp our own identity. We are constantly asking ourselves, 'What kind of person do I want to be?' By modeling ourselves after people we admire, we come closer to discovering who we really are."

For an American Culture class in high school, Phil wrote a personal history paper, in which he was to name the most important influences in his life. Seeing the movie *Star Wars*, he had written, was one. At first, I dismissed his claim. Leave it to Phil, I thought, to think a movie the highlight of his life. But, as I watched Joseph Campbell's television series *The Power of Myth* a year or so later, I learned that *Star Wars* is the archetypal story of the hero's journey.

Phil saw the first *Star Wars* movie at least three times, and he was captivated. The world of science fiction offered a mysterious, unbounded flight for the imagination, an alternative to the well-worn, mundane paths of a daily school routine. The film depicted speed and rockets, interplanetary travel and supersonic weapons. He played by the hour with plastic replicas of the spaceships and action figures. How many times, I wondered, had he cast himself in the role of Luke Skywalker? How many times had he saved Princess Leia?

At fifteen, Phil sent away for a catalogue from NOLS, the National Outdoor Leadership School. He knew right away which program he wanted to do: Wind River Mountaineering. The minimum age was sixteen, but he begged and called the school, and they relented, making an exception to the rule. I was mystified. I had never even learned to downhill ski. I appreciated the beauty of mountains, but their heights terrified me. Now my son was going to climb one. While he was gone that summer, as I waited in a receiving line at a wedding, a friend told me he had just heard about a teenager killed on a similar adventure program, knocked off the mountain by a falling boulder. Phil returned safely, energized, hooked on climbing.

The next summer, he begged to climb again. He researched and found a climbing school in the Pacific Northwest. We checked the school out with a mountaineering friend of ours, who said it was legitimate, but a month before Phil was to leave, they called to say no one else had signed up for Phil's particular trip. Would he like to come anyway, to climb one-on-one with the guide? I agonized again, but his desire to climb was so strong that I felt it needed to be honored, supported, even encouraged. We put him on a plane alone, bound for Washington to climb with an utter stranger, to summit Mount Baker. I waited fearfully at home. He returned again, this time with photographs of himself dangling from ropes over an icy crevasse, spread-eagle on rock faces, standing triumphant on a summit.

In his last year of high school, Phil and his friend Dryw had spent their final quarter on a special independent project: tracing the footsteps of Mark Twain's journey west—on bicycle. They spent weeks pedaling across the Great Plains, then climbing up and over the Rocky Mountains to the Pacific Ocean.

For Phil, climbing became part of his identity, something that set him apart from his Minnesota peers. He bought issues of *Rock and Ice* and *Climbing* magazines, read anthologies like *Mountain Journeys* and *Why I Climb*. When it came time in senior year for the dreaded college admissions essay, he sent Bates College these words about climbing: "First, I delight in living on the edge, echoing Plato's 'the unrisked life is not worth living.' I tend not to think of accidents or of dying on a climb," he wrote. "I think I'd probably give up climbing if I did. I am an optimist. I try to look at the fear involved with a climb as an obstacle which makes meeting the challenge more enjoyable."

One night in July 1992—hot, thick, the ceiling fan turning, churning, having little impact—Angus and I were getting ready for bed. The fantasies were starting up again, the apocalyptic visions that plagued me. Phil had finished his freshman year at Bates. He was out west again, on a second NOLS course to learn about field observation in the mountains. Virtually no climbing was involved, but I was imagining disaster. This time it was a lightning strike. I could see it in my mind's eye: the storm, the wind, the small band of wilderness campers. I could see the angry bolt zap, then imagine it catching Phil and his pack, see him hit the ground. I covered my eyes with my hands, leaned over, trying to push the thoughts away. I looked at Angus, deciding this time to tell him.

"Sometimes,—no, lots of times," I said, "I have these ominous thoughts about Phil. Disasters. Of all kinds. It drives me crazy. I'm so worried."

He looked at me, serious, he who never worried. "You shouldn't think that way," he said. "Patterns like that can be dangerous. Thinking like that might even create it at some level, conjure it out of nowhere. He'll be fine. Now come to bed."

Once, when Phil was a toddler, I had left him briefly sitting in the bathtub to answer the door or the phone or something. I ran quickly back to the bathroom, only to find Phil slumped over, his face in the water, his blond hair floating, radiating like a silver dandelion out around him. I yelled, grabbed him by the hair, and pulled up with all my might.

"Ow, Mommy, ouch!" He burst into tears. He had been fine, just playing, holding his breath under water, blowing bubbles. After that, I had several drowning dreams: images of Phil floating, gray. I would wake up devastated.

I remember too that cold November day, just after Thanksgiving, the year Phil was six. Angus had been watching the lake anxiously for a couple of weeks, just as he did every year at that time, praying that it wouldn't snow. At first the ice was just a ruffled collar around the shore, a delicate shelf onto which ducks were barely light enough to scramble without breaking through. Then one morning: no more ripples. The surface was congealed, just rigid enough to resist a steady, quiet breeze. Small boys scooped large stones from the shore, heaved them like shot put out onto the new ice, lay bets as to whether they would break through or skim several feet to a halt. The season became a waiting game: willing the clouds back, forbidding snow. That year it was cold—biting cold. We had no snow for days, even a week and more, until the whole lake was thick, a skating rink as smooth and black as a phonograph record. Angus had recruited Walter Barry and Stew to join us. We all laced on skates and took off.

The early evening sky glowed mother-of-pearl overhead. The ice was dark and clear; we could see by the cracks that the ice was a couple of inches thick—easily strong enough to bear our human weight. We skated off, drifting far from one another. I was absorbed, watching my feet make swirls, etching chalk messages to summer sunfish freeze-framed, unaware of life above their underwater world. Suddenly a shout. My eyes swept the gray horizon to a far-off place, a patch of open water, a pair of small arms waving, splashing high. "It's Phil!" someone yelled.

The words echoed through a bell chamber, as if I was suddenly encased in glass. My pulse fell out of rhythm, my legs turned to lead as waves of terror shuddered up my spine. I stood, utterly immobile, breath suspended. I watched Angus, with Walter at his heels, streak directly toward the hole, legs pumping, hockey sticks in hand. They lay down on the ice, Angus at the edge of the hole, Walter behind him holding his legs. With stick and arm outstretched, he coaxed his step-son gently, firmly, calmly. Phil had just learned to swim the past summer, but he was logy, weighed down by his skates and heavy snowsuit. The ice kept breaking off in pieces, the shelf above that underwater spring too thin to hold. At last Phil grabbed the handle tight with mittened hands. They pulled—a mighty heave—and he was out. My heart could beat again.

As we skated home, the edges of my brain congealed around the questions, some that echo still like sonic ice booms underfoot: if Angus had failed, would I, could I have tried the rescue? Could I have ever given up? We had both only been divorced two years and married to each other a year and a half. What would death have done then to love, to trust, to marriage?

"Did you ever worry about me?" I asked my own mother once. "I mean about my driving home when I was a teenager, or when I was away in the Peace Corps?"

"Never." She was clear, definite. "I mean no—I never worried about you. Not at all!" I knew she loved me, utterly, unconditionally. Until then, I had assumed that all mothers were haunted by these images of apocalypse, that they just came with the mental geography of parenthood. In some ways, I thought some protective force might be behind them. By imagining the worst, I could keep disaster at bay, demystify it, even intimidate it into submission. More of me, though, believed Angus was right: these patterns of thought should be banished. I also knew that Phil was careful, skilled. His friends had all told me that he was the only one of their gang who refused even to move his car until everyone had his seat belt buckled. So I steered my thinking in new directions, forced the thoughts down, vaporized the fantasies.

But the anxiety bubbling underneath the surface shaped my relationship with my son. I never told Phil about the phantoms.

CHAPTER 4

Facing Off

Children are by far more clever in a power contest.
They aren't inhibited by social consequences of
"appearances" or dangerous consequences of their
actions.

Rudolf Dreikurs

Phil knew—he always knew—how much I loved him, but it did not
keep us from facing off, engaging in the inevitable power plays of parenting. From the terrible twos and the horrible fours, through childhood and beyond, the even-numbered years were the worst. Over the
smallest challenges to my authority, I would sometimes feel like
killing Phil, this person I loved most in the world.

The game of push and pull intensified in adolescence, beginning
when Phil was in junior high. After one of those Lake Superior jaunts
that included the cliff jumping, I picked up—as mothers often do—the
hint that beer was a feature of the annual weekend. I never thought it
accompanied the jumping, but the two were related nonetheless: a
surefire technique to lift those young, easy spirits, bouncing them on
billows of laughter, an adventure as memorable as a hurl into space.

As the years went on, teenage drinking became an issue that
plagued our parenting. We knew that beer was at the weekend parties,
rumored to be in houses where the parents were out of town. We

talked often with Phil, expressing our disapproval of alcohol at his age, begging him to buck the peer pressure and abstain. Phil never denied that he participated in these debaucheries. He would listen respectfully to our pleas, protest, but obligingly stay home when a specific incident that had come to our attention would result in his being grounded for the weekend.

When he and his friends began to drive, the stakes rose. *"Never,"* we insisted, "never drive if you've been drinking." We seemed to command his attention on that one, and the dynamic shifted. Now we received late-night phone calls asking to spend the night at a friend's house. We were torn, sure that alcohol was involved but relieved that he wouldn't be driving or taking a ride with an inebriated friend. Was our praise for his car judgment tacit approval for the drinking that preceded it? More talks would ensue, and progress was elusive.

The most disturbing aspect was that Phil and his friends didn't just take an occasional sip. They drank, he told us, to get drunk; that was part of the allure, the "rush" a good portion of the thrill. Angus and I drink alcohol regularly. We rarely choose hard liquor, but few days go by that we don't have a couple of glasses of wine with our dinner. Preaching against alcohol is hard when you regularly drink yourself. Were we setting a bad example? We continued to live our lives, simultaneously telling Phil we did not condone his underage drinking. We continued to levy consequences when we found out he had broken the rules.

Phil's school encouraged all the parents to take a workshop that instructed us on the dangers of alcohol and the warning signs of addiction. We were concerned, carefully applying the criteria we had learned, but Phil didn't fit the profile of an addict. He was consistently open and truthful when we questioned him about his behavior, not secretive. He eagerly signed up for month-long wilderness outings with NOLS, where chemicals of any kind were strictly forbidden. Still, he and his friends clearly drank too much, probably at levels that were dangerous to their young minds and bodies.

Toward the end of senior year, Phil and his friend Dryw were scheduled to make an assembly presentation about their senior project, the bicycle trip they had taken from Minneapolis to California. I was sitting in the audience, eager to hear what they had to say, when there was a delay and some mysterious shuffling in the hall. I stepped outside the auditorium to find that Phil had not arrived, which was not like him at all. While Dryw went on to do the program alone, I nervously left to look for my son. I found him at home, anxious and scared. "I just freaked out," he told me. "I hadn't prepared very well. When I got to school, I couldn't get out of the car. I've been driving around this whole time wondering what hit me."

The school was so surprised at this uncharacteristically erratic behavior that they requested we have Phil assessed by a counselor to see whether alcohol and chemicals might have played a role in the incident. He went willingly, insisting that he had just experienced an anxiety attack, that alcohol had nothing to do with it. After the tests and interviews, the consultant's conclusion was the same as ours: he probably drank too much in social situations but was not addicted.

Did the love of risk, the need for thrill, go hand in hand with a tendency to spice up everyday life with artificial highs? Were they an inevitable combination? I didn't know. I just prayed he would temper his behavior as he grew older.

We had our share of everyday struggles, but the central battlefield on which Phil and I met time and again was school. From the beginning, I had thought my son was smart. He talked early. He was an energetic, verbal child who loved books. In his second year—when other children his age crawled, walked, and explored—he loved to be read to, would sit in my lap or on the floor for hours paging through a large glossy book called *Busytown*. He would examine each tiny picture: the mail carrier delivering mail, the baseball player swinging a bat, the mechanic in the repair shop. He remembered them all and asked questions constantly.

In school, he seemed to perform to everyone's expectations. The reports from his day care center, then later the public Montessori school, all said he was a pleasure to have in class. He worked hard, made good progress. I had always been a good student myself. I found school easy, for the most part. I too had worked hard; I did well. I loved watching Phil repeat this pattern. I praised his good performance lavishly, believing that a strong self-concept would be his most valuable tool.

Then, in fourth grade, Angus and I decided to send him to a private school, the same one we had both attended from eighth grade to graduation. After the entrance tests, I sat back and waited for the call, assuming Phil would be automatically accepted, but the scores were not what I'd thought they'd be. However one determines IQ at eight years old, Phil had tested at a resoundingly average level. In reading and math both, when compared with other independent-school kids, he fell well below the top quartile. I received a call from the school, saying they wanted to retest Phil in spelling. His results had suggested the possibility of a learning disability. "No," I said. "We'll bring him in again, but his Montessori school just didn't put an emphasis on spelling. They were afraid it would stifle creativity." Indeed, they ruled out dyslexia and other disorders. He qualified for the new school, but just barely. I never told him that, wanting to keep his self-concept high. I sent him off, confident that he would be fine, half assuming the tests had been wrong.

Phil did fine at first. His lower-school reports showed decent performance, enthusiasm for learning. His teachers loved him and glowed in their comments. Beginning in sixth grade, however, when he entered the middle school, I began to see signs that troubled me. Quarterly reports often noted that Phil talked in class and distracted other students; he occasionally turned homework assignments in late. A couple of teachers felt he was not working up to his potential. By the time he reached high school, this pattern had become established. Phil was erratic, distracted. He continued to act up, talking in class, particularly with teachers whom he disliked.

At home our rules were clear: no television on weeknights, no after-dinner choice but to go to his room to study. Once in his room, however, behind the closed door, he ruled. He set up a basketball hoop over his wastebasket and lobbed paper balls by the hour. He wore earphones and boogied his way around the room, spent hours paging through bicycle and climbing magazines, talking on the phone, and trying on clothes.

I wasn't sure whether he was in over his head, whether perhaps the school's rigorous academic program exceeded his abilities, but no—the faculty reassured me that he could do better if he set his mind to it. Now and then, maybe one quarter every year, Phil would turn over a new leaf. Motivation would return. He would conscientiously turn down the music, turn in his assignments, and turn out B's and B+'s. Then, just as we were beginning to think we were home free, the distraction and inattentiveness would return, the maddening attitude that didn't try and didn't care.

By then, I was a trustee of the school. I wanted more than anything for Phil to succeed, to excel, to make me proud. His father, his stepfather, and I had all been hard workers and student leaders in high school. Why didn't he fit the mold? Where was this resistance coming from? College was just around the corner. Didn't he want to get into a good school? Sometimes I would look at him and think he was from a foreign country.

On my birthday, in November of Phil's sophomore year, I found this letter, written on yellow legal-pad paper, on my plate at dinner:

Dear Mom:

Sadly, because of pure incompetence on the part of your son, there will be no birthday present from me except what is written on this parchment.

To begin: I know that over the last period of time, I haven't been acting my nicest towards you. What I want you to know is that I totally realize this fact. It's just that I'm at the age when it's very hard for me to be nice because of my yearning for more and more independence. Now I know this mean attitude from me doesn't make you feel very good. But I want you to know that it hurts me just as much when I'm mean to you. Every time I ignore you or yell at you, I'm only wishing I could do just the opposite, but something inside me keeps me from being nice. Hopefully, this stage in my life will soon pass, but for now though, I want you to know that I still consider you my mom and I care about you very much. Although I don't show this, if you could see inside me, you could see that being mean is just a part of growing up and the older I get, the nicer I become. So with that, I will wish you a very happy birthday and a wonderful year of being 43.

Love,

your son, Phil

This was always the turn it took. I would realize, finally, what a self-aware, thoughtful person he was at heart. Moves like this melted my heart and made me remember that it was *his* life he was leading after all, not mine.

Phil did get nicer as he grew older, as the adolescent hormones began to settle down. I still felt that his school performance—or lack thereof—was an ongoing statement of revolt, his report cards a kind of personal manifesto that put me in my place and staked out a territory beyond my control. He tested adequately on the SATs and eked out a final record that—combined with a better-than-average extracurricular performance, interview, and personal recommendations—landed him at Bates College in Maine, a small liberal arts school that was perfect for the kind of support he needed.

Once Phil was away from home, out from under our expectations, he took his academic struggles into his own hands. He came home Christmas vacation the first year and announced, "There is something

wrong with me. I can't sit in the library and study for three hours like
the other kids, Mom. I just can't concentrate like they do." Indeed, his
first semester he had received two D's and two B's. I wrote it off, saw
this as more of his same old pattern, but he came home for the summer more determined than ever. "I want to be tested to see if there's
something wrong with me."

We found a consultant with the help of Phil's old high school
counselors and had him put through an extensive evaluation with a
battery of tests. When we met with the consultants to hear their con-
clusions, I was flabbergasted. Phil had a clear case of Attention Deficit
Disorder without Hyperactivity. The "TOVA" test, a measure of
variables of attention, had clearly recorded a neurological glitch, a
tiny lag in moving a signal from one particular part of the brain to
another, a slight rhythmic discord that had consequences in his ability to concentrate. The syndrome was fairly common, we were told,
and the consultant catalogued a cluster of behaviors that often accom-
pany the disorder: distractibility, lack of concentration, a tendency to
lose things and to forget things, an attraction to physically daring
activities. Phil—like many kids with the syndrome—had learned to
survive on his considerable interpersonal and oral skills; when it came
to reading and extended study, he had clearly been at a disadvantage.
This syndrome only affected school, they told us. Once he was out of
an academic setting, he would choose an appropriate career path, and
the ADD wouldn't be an issue anymore.

How could we have gone so long without identifying the problem? If the cluster of behaviors was so predictable, why hadn't it
occurred to his high school counselors to have him tested? I was confused and angry in retrospect—especially at myself for having written
off his performance problems as mere adolescent rebellion. I was
proud of Phil for having taken charge of his own life.

Phil returned to Bates for his sophomore year. He had with him a
prescription for a low dose of Ritalin to take when he needed to concentrate for long periods of time. He had a list of recommendations

for approaches to study that would be appropriate for his learning style. His grades began to improve, and—more importantly—his interest, confidence, and motivation soared. The turnaround was not complete, however. He did become frustrated and decide to take time off for a semester in Seattle, but when he returned for his last two semesters at Bates, he poured himself heart and soul into his environmental studies curriculum.

CHAPTER 5

From the Head to the Heart

We cannot live the afternoon of life according to the programme of life's morning; for what was great in the morning will be little at evening, and what in the morning was true will at evening have become a lie.

C. G. Jung

An evening in November 1991: I am forty-six, and I am with a group from my confirmation class gathered in St. Mark's sanctuary. My new friends, two men and a woman on the clerical staff, have changed into white robes, tied with a rope sash. The robes signal that we have crossed over into a new realm, from the head to the heart. Along with another man in the group, I am here to be baptized. I am sure of my decision, but I am still a little afraid. Angus is with me, but not our children, not my parents. This moment is a private one for me, one that I still feel embarrassed about out in the world.

We lift our prayer books and begin the service of Holy Baptism. The dean looks at me. "Do you renounce Satan and all the spiritual forces of wickedness that rebel against God?" What is this? I think.

How absurd! I don't believe in "Satan," in the devil, and my God isn't some kind of tyrant you can rebel against. I feel the rush of protest, the voices rising from my brain, out of my head, a loud chorus of skepticism, of rationality, logic, and judgment.

"I renounce them!" I hear myself saying to silence the din. "I renounce them!" I renounce whatever might keep me from this path of discovery, of inner peace, of deep reward. I renounce them: the doubts, the history tests, the need for proof, the need for science. This journey is one of the heart, one of poetry, wisdom, and ancient story. As I take the body, the Communion wafer, as I drink the wine, the blood of Christ, I feel sure—not of what I believe, but of the road I have chosen to travel.

I learned, as my spirit began to wake up, that the path from the head to the heart is arduous—steep, overgrown, and lengthened with switchbacks. With my family background and my overdeveloped left brain, I seemingly had to learn to walk all over again. The core of the journey was just plain practice. I continued to take yoga, and I began to study *pranayama*, a yogic breathing discipline. The breathing patterns became a kind of meditation that grounded me each day, turned me into a sponge, ready to absorb the lessons of the path. I went to church just about every week, and I met regularly with the bishop, who became a trusted mentor and friend.

Then there was Nancy, who had been my best friend all through high school. We had gone east to college together, and we had kept up the relationship, meeting regularly for lunch during all the years of our adult lives. She had grown up in the Congregational Church. She had been active in its youth groups and now, as an adult, she served as a trustee. When she was in her late thirties—before any of this interest in the sacred had begun to stir in me—she enrolled at a local seminary and earned a degree in counseling. She was becoming a professional spiritual director.

At first, her new vocation annoyed me. Her language changed, and I felt alienated as she became obsessed with issues of spirit. We continued to meet for lunch, but I was worried that this new direction threatened to ruin our friendship. She never tried to force me to see things her way, but as I began to open up myself—to "thaw out," as she put it—she became a valuable guide. She understood everything I was saying. She was well-read, insightful, and she encouraged me to keep exploring, to keep growing.

Books had been part of my quest from the very start. M. Scott Peck's *The Road Less Traveled*, Joseph Campbell's *The Power of Myth*, and Ken Wilber's *No Boundary* had all led to revelation. When Phil was in his junior year in high school, I signed up to go to school myself. I enrolled that February in a Masters in Liberal Studies program at Hamline, a local university, which was seemingly a crazy thing to do. I knew this quest wasn't a rational process, that the academic world was probably the last place I should turn, but I needed the change of pace that study would provide. I needed to step out for a while, out of the world of board meetings, fundraising, and even too many social events. School provided just the excuse I needed.

Once there, I found myself drawn to religion and writing classes. Hamline was flexible about accepting credits from other area schools, so I signed up for a year-long course in the history of Christian spirituality at a nearby Catholic women's college. I wanted to start at the beginning, to go back in time, to read the original saints and wisdom figures who had written about their experience of God. I wanted to absorb their words directly, to see whether their insights and observations had any relationship to the things I was discovering. I wanted to hone my own inner path using the tools of others' hard-won struggles.

We read men and women from the fifth century to the twentieth, tracing the development of a religion and a church, but chronicled in personal experience and reflection. In Augustine's *Confessions*, for example, then later Thomas Merton's *Seven Storey Mountain*, I read other conversion stories like mine. *The Rule of St. Benedict* helped me in the process of restoring balance to my life, to feel right about the new priority I had placed on contemplation and study, to see that I had become too outwardly drawn into action and community.

Reading Julian of Norwich showed me how to put a name to what I had been through in my divorce. At the time, the similarities never occurred to me, but I could now begin to see that the story of Christ's passion—his death and resurrection—mirrored my own way through pain and suffering into a new marriage and new life. I could see how the rhythm of the church year was reflected in so many life situations and how it could be of value to Christians to teach them to hope when things seemed blackest.

Martin Luther and Dorothy Day both wrote about the spiritual life in action. They helped me to consider my own talents and inclinations and what it would mean for me to give back to the world. I worried that I never seemed attracted to working in a homeless shelter or a soup kitchen. I wondered if I could still be a Christian if I didn't do that kind of work. Luther and Day gave me permission to consider my own unique gifts, to see that each of us is different and that I should tune my ear carefully to discover my own personal vocation.

My favorite mystic was Meister Eckhart, a thirteenth-century German monk and priest. His words—his sermons and writings as he traveled from monastery to monastery—allowed me to find my way to God. He, like me, rejected the notion of an anthropomorphic deity, one who was a man or a person with thoughts and feelings like human beings. I was excited to find in reading Eckhart a God I was comfortable with, a "pure, form-free being of divine unity." This God was an infinite mystery without qualities, without boundaries, even without a name. Eckhart wrote of the kind of prayer I had been drawn to, one of pure receptivity, silence, and stillness: the *Via Negativa*, the path of inwardness. I realized, in reading Eckhart and later the Quakers, that the meditation I had discovered in the Eastern and yogic practices has a long history and tradition in Christianity. Meditation had attracted me since this whole process of awakening had begun. Prayer felt right to me in silence, in a relaxation pose at the end of yoga class, in the breathing exercises called *pranayama* that I was beginning to practice daily.

My meditation practice began one summer when I woke each day with the birds before anyone else was up. I would sit alone in the half light, faithfully breathing slowly in and out in patterns that required all my attention in order not to lose the rhythm. When I was finished, I felt so calm, so centered, that I began to stay on my cushion just a while longer, to repeat just one phrase slowly, silently, in order to keep that focus inside. Staying focused was very hard at times. My mind wandered; fantasies and memories drew me away. But I was determined to see what I could discover in the practice, so I kept at it until those morning sessions became an essential part of my day.

Many of the mystics and sages I was reading had tried to articulate and describe the path of spiritual progress. How does it go forward, and what is needed to reach what might be called enlightenment or unity with God? One of those authors puzzled me mightily: the sixteenth-century Spanish monk and poet called John of the Cross. His book *The Dark Night* was a detailed road map of the spiritual journey, the stages that a seeker like myself would be likely to encounter. He described the many foibles of the spiritual neophyte—all of which described me to a T—then he went on to chronicle the "dark nights" of the senses and of the soul, stages that any serious seeker had to experience. He described these stages as devastating bouts of spiritual dryness, of emptiness, of despair, doubt, and pain, all of which he said were necessary in order to evolve spiritually. I read his words with stubborn resistance. I couldn't imagine that they applied to me. So far, the spiritual life had offered me the experience of an expanded spirit, a love of sacred music and scripture, the deep peace of silence and contemplative prayer. I figured that the upheaval of this turning, the occasional tears I had shed at the mystery of it all, would be a dark enough night for me. I had given religion such a deliberate welcome, a willing embrace. I was clearly on the cosmic fast track. Surely I would be spared John's dark night of the soul.

I had kept a journal in the History of Christian Spirituality class, and now I was working on it, expanding it, turning it into my master's thesis. I was spending long hours writing at the computer. One afternoon, Phil appeared in the room I used for an office. He was home for spring vacation from Bates, and he was curious to know what I was doing in there for so long. He knew I had been going through some sort of spiritual awakening, and he worried at times that I would become a new person, someone he didn't recognize or couldn't predict.

Phil was raised as I had been, in a secular household. All the years the kids had been growing up, our Sunday mornings had been spent around a dining-room table laid with pancakes and maple syrup. None of the four children—Angus's three or Phil—had ever been baptized. While they were young, we never went to church. The only exception was Christmas Eve. We would all bundle up—as many of us as could be recruited in a given year—and drive through the frigid night to St. Mark's. There we would absorb the pageantry of the late-night service, the procession, the bells, the colorful vestments and exquisite music. I thrilled to the exotic ritual, but in those days, church was just another Christmas tradition, on a par with roast beef, Yorkshire pudding, the stockings, the tree, and the mound of presents. Typically Phil fell asleep on my lap, and we sneaked out before Communion.

Now here I was, off on a brand-new tack, one for which Phil had never been prepared. I could see that, for him, the world of wilderness and adventure filled his soul. He wouldn't have called it "spiritual," but I could see that climbing, for example, fed his hunger for mystical experience. As "awesome" became a staple of his vocabulary, I could see that he and his generation needed to be reminded of their own insignificance, of their connection with the infinite. In the essay that was part of his application to Bates, he wrote about what mountain climbers call the "white moment"—the "overwhelming feeling you experience immediately after reaching the summit. It's as if your whole body is overcome with satisfaction. All other aspects of life are blurred. . . ." Reading those words in Phil's essay excited me. I felt I was witnessing the expression of a budding spiritual awareness, one that held the potential for receptivity, and one that could grow and be nurtured in the distant future.

That afternoon, Phil asked if he could read what I had been writing, an early draft of my thesis, a journal of a year in which each chapter focused on a Christian wisdom figure, followed by reflections on my own life prompted by their words. He came back a few hours later. He said he liked the writing. He felt privileged to read so much personal revelation, to learn so much about his mother's inner life, but the religion part was off the wall.

"This is fine for you, Mom," he said, dropping the manuscript in my lap, "but whatever you do, don't try to get me into it." He started for the door.

"Don't worry. I wouldn't dream of it," I replied quickly.

He asked what I meant.

"You're too young. I mean it, Phil. This has meant so much to me in my forties. I'm at a more reflective, quiet phase of my life. I have time to slow down, to think deeply about these things. There will be plenty of opportunity for you to find your own path some day. You've got other things to think about. Don't even think about it now."

Phil was majoring in environmental studies at Bates. He had wanted to study ecology in all its aspects—the interconnectedness of the natural world, the threats to planet Earth from our industrial age, our material lifestyle, the social and political challenges we face in trying to change both the culture and our personal and corporate behavior.

One day that spring, after Phil had returned to school after vacation, he called home, bubbling over with enthusiasm. He had participated in a workshop as part of an environmental education class. The workshop had included a "Council of All Beings," a deep ecology ritual to help humans move beyond their anthropocentric and exploitative mind-set in relation to our natural world. The workshop began with an exercise in which the students told their stories—of love of the wilderness and of loss—of their pain at what is happening to that world. They were inspired by Thich Nhat Hanh's words: "What we need most to do is to hear within ourselves the sounds of the Earth crying." They each made a mask and came back to the "council" as a representative of an endangered species now facing extinction: the whooping crane, the howler monkey, the spotted owl. All the students spoke, letting the species speak through them, articulating their gifts to the planet. They danced around a fire, then—one by one—they threw the masks into the fire, releasing the life forms and honoring and thanking them as they burst into flames.

The ceremony had power for Phil. The ritual fire had sparked a passion I had not heard in him before. He bought a copy of the book written by the workshop's leaders and sent it home to me. He was burning with energy, devotion to the ecological cause, and an irrepressible new curiosity. At the end of the year, he told me he had signed up for not one, but *four* religion classes for the following semester. I was astounded. All I had done was to tell him he was too young for it. He had set out to prove me wrong, and I had to admit he was succeeding.

The next fall he returned to Bates and plunged into his classes with gusto: Environmentalism in Christian Thought, Anthropological Approaches to the Study of Religion, Philosophy of Religion, and the Buddhist Tradition. He petitioned a faculty committee and received permission to change his major from environmental studies to "eco-spirituality." Second semester he took three more classes: Introduction to the New Testament, Ascetic and Monastic

Christianity, and the Study of Religion, a survey course he needed for his new major. The bulk of his time was devoted to writing his senior thesis: *Consider the Lilies: Toward a Theology for the Earth.*

Aware that Christianity had been accused of preaching an ambiguous message toward the earth and had often been blamed for the contemporary ecological crisis, Phil set out to uncover valuable, nature-affirming strains that had always existed within the Christian tradition and had been habitually overlooked. He wanted to envision a new Christian-based theology for the earth. He searched the Old and New Testaments to find the roots of a theology of nature. He constructed a portrait of an environmental Jesus based on the words of the Gospels. He examined the life and works of St. Francis, the thirteenth-century nature theologian. Finally, he formulated a moving vision for a "Creation Order," a new future for Christianity that would communicate a modern-day environmental message and make us responsible stewards of the natural world. While his paper was academic and had the serious, earnest overtones of any undergraduate thesis, nonetheless Phil's own love for the wilderness came through its pages: "The smell of clean air, that is good; the towering majesty of a lodge pole pine, that is good; and the comforting sound of a running river. . . . What better way to discover God," he wrote, "than by sitting in quiet meditation above a cascading alpine waterfall?"

His journey and mine were not the same, nor were they working on the same timetable, but I could see he was sincere, and I was excited to watch where it would all lead.

CHAPTER 6

Phil's Women

Til I loved
I never lived—Enough.

Emily Dickinson

In spring 1995, Phil was full of energy, sure of what he wanted to do. He had completed all the requirements for his major at Bates, but he still had a number of credits to complete, classes he had missed during the semester he took off to work in Seattle. His own college class was graduating, so he wanted to finish elsewhere. He applied to Lewis and Clark College in Portland, Oregon, and was accepted for the following fall. Then he set out to find a summer job. He went to Washington and interviewed with the National Park Service and the Student Conservation Association. He wanted to work in the wilderness, hopefully somewhere in the mountains where he could climb.

Several weeks later, Phil called me. He had learned he was a finalist for a student internship at Mount Rainier National Park, a dream job for him. He had the phone number of the woman who would make the final decision. "Should I call her, Mom?" he asked. "I don't want to bug her, but I want to try to convince her to take me."

Inside, I clenched. I wanted him to spend the summer safe at home, near me. Why didn't I just advise him to get a desk job in Minneapolis, that it would be better for his résumé, more important for his future? But the air was crackling with his excitement, and I could feel his longing. So I said instead, "Go for it, Phil. Call her. I'll bet it will make a difference if she knows you really want the job."

They hired Phil for the internship at Mount Rainier. He was ecstatic. In June, he came home on his way west to Washington. His friend Nicole, who was traveling to her own job in Sun Valley, Idaho, was with him. I had already met Nicole, out in Seattle during Phil's semester off, and I was eager to see her again.

In fact, I had always liked the women in Phil's life. He was rarely without romantic interest as he grew. In junior high, he went to swimming parties and movies on Saturday afternoons. He told me, much to my surprise, about his first kiss, a fellow junior counselor on the dock at Camp Kici Yapi. In high school, the stakes rose, but no one was particularly special until Elizabeth.

Elizabeth had long, thick honey-colored hair and a sprinkle of freckles on her nose, just like he did. She was a year older than Phil and slightly out of reach, but he was clearly smitten. She was sixteen, old enough to drive; he was still on a bike. From her point of view, the relationship couldn't work. A year later, they were a couple. They took long walks around the lake near our house, talked for hours on the phone, spent at least one evening a weekend in each other's company. Because of their age difference, their friends did not always mesh, so they spent lots of time alone together. I liked Elizabeth. I was happy for Phil, but I began to wonder whether their relationship would lead to a physical intimacy that was premature.

Elizabeth graduated, then went off to Connecticut College in the fall. They wrote letters constantly. He begged to be allowed to visit her for her birthday early in March, and I refused. "But *why* can't I go?" he wheedled.

"For lots of reasons," I replied. "You would have to miss school. It's too much to spend on travel. Don't forget our family vacation is coming up a couple of weeks later. And besides, it just isn't appropriate at your age."

One day, in the midst of this continuing argument, he slipped a folded piece of paper under my bedroom door. "Dear Mom," began the letter I have kept all these years. "I am writing you this because I am too furious to talk. . . ." The missive was a carefully constructed response to each of my reasons, in categories: money (he would find a way to pay for it himself), school (he had the assistant principal's permission to take time off), and maturity (he had already traveled alone and stayed overnight at a college). "So," he wrote,

it must be staying with Elizabeth—S-E-X!! (I'm sure there are other reasons but I think this is the one that's really eating you.) I don't imagine this will do any good to tell but I might as well— You probably have no idea about my sex life, or maybe you do. Yes, Elizabeth and I have sex together. But let me assure you that we're always very careful and use protection and all that. And if I were to go there for the weekend, it wouldn't be the first time I have slept with her. I hope this isn't too shocking—I don't think it is. Elizabeth and I are deeply in love—something I see you don't totally realize. You may laugh this statement off, but please give it some thought, and I am completely confident that I am old and mature enough to handle a weekend alone.

So my fears were legitimate. I looked at the paper again, this precious offering of truth, so rare in these years of closed doors and tight-lipped teenage silence. How could I not reward such openness, such honesty? I tried to picture him—my son, my baby—actually engaged in sexual intercourse. I thought back on my own high school years, the hours spent making out in the basement with my boyfriend,

adhering to clear, mutually accepted boundaries. Sex at Phil's age was
too much, too soon.

I went to his room and paused, face-to-face with Magic Johnson
taped to the outside of the closed door. I knocked.

"Mom?"

I opened the door and walked in. He was sitting in his desk chair
pulled up to the window, his back to me, sucking a giant lollipop. He
looked the same, but my eye selected the details a little differently: the
shoulders were broad now, the blond hair beginning to darken,
crimped where it faded into short sideburns around the ears. The
jeans fit like a man's, not a child's, a worn outline of a wallet on the
back pocket, a smoothness where they stretched over muscular thighs
and calves.

"Thanks for the letter, Phil. I have to admit, I *was* kind of wondering."

"So now can I go?"

I loved him. I understood his passion and his need, but I couldn't
imagine sending this seventeen-year-old off on a weekend tryst. Elizabeth would be home in a matter of weeks.

"No."

"But *why?*"

"For all the reasons I've already given you."

He exploded in rage, hurling the lollipop against the wall and
splintering it into a thousand pieces on the carpet. More fierce words
came, more protestations. He pushed and shoved his will against my
power. Hating this rift between us, I held on tight.

But Phil knew how to move on. Once he had released the anger,
the storm was over. He made a video to send off to Connecticut in his
stead. The tape was a detailed chronicle of a snowy February day,
from the moment of waking up to going to sleep, and he asked each
person he encountered—family, friends, teachers—to "say happy
birthday to Elizabeth." At the end, that evening before bed, he turned
the tape on himself. Sitting in a white wicker chair set up under an

indoor tree, a neat crewneck sweater over a plaid shirt, he looked directly into the camera. The twinkle in his eye was there, the little smile at the corner of his mouth. "I would just like to say that I love you very much, I miss you, and I can't wait to see you in a couple of weeks."

Their relationship was rocky at times. Elizabeth took a semester off for soul-searching during her sophomore year. Eventually they began to drift apart.

"Elizabeth dumped me again," said Phil, sitting on the front stairs one day, tears rolling down cheeks just beginning to manifest sparse blond stubble. My heart went out to this son of mine. I wanted it to work for his sake, but I knew he needed to move on with his life. Their relationship ended, petered out really, in fits and starts. For months, years even, the mention of her name or a glimpse of her visiting her friend next door would prompt a nostalgic longing. He was always open about it, never embarrassed to let me know of his vulnerability. At least, I thought, he has survived his first love affair with his pride intact.

Now, with Nicole, Phil seemed to have settled into a mature relationship. Back in December of his junior year at Bates, after having just missed being accepted by an environmental program in Costa Rica, Phil had had enough of school. He wanted to take a semester off, to live and work in Seattle. "No school, no money," we said, but he was determined to follow through.

One January day in 1994, Phil drove west in a blinding blizzard accompanied by his roommate Jeff. They announced that a third roommate would be flying out from Boston to join them "just to help pay the rent." Her name was Nicole. "She's a knockout, Mom, but I really don't know her very well; we're just friends," he had said when I expressed surprise that he would have a female roommate.

All three of them landed jobs, Phil at a pizza joint on the shores of a lake, and somehow, collectively and responsibly, they eked out a living. About six weeks into the adventure, I received a call. "Nicole and I are kind of into each other now," he announced. Uh oh, I thought to myself, he probably means it literally. . . . We flew out for a visit several weeks later.

Nicole was out for a run when we arrived, but I remember looking into her bedroom, my eye running curiously over an obviously current pile of books by her bed: Toni Morrison, Jeanette Winterson . . . Hmmm, I thought, interesting books. . . . I think I'm going to like this young woman.

Minutes later, Nicole returned, breathless, in shorts and an oversized T-shirt. She was small with an athletic body, her ruddy cheeks flushed from her jog. Her eyes were bright and eager, her dimpled smile friendly and natural. She had shoulder-length dark brown hair tucked behind her ears. Over dinner that night in a restaurant, we began to get acquainted. She told us about her summer place in Maine, her parents, her two brothers (all of whom Phil had met and loved in brief outings away from Bates to visit them), about her internship editing the Sierra Club newsletter and her part-time stint waiting on tables to help make ends meet. We took them to a grocery store the next day and made heroes of ourselves with a shopping cart full of food: jam (a large-sized jar), steak and cookies for him, frozen veggie burgers for her, a bunch of daffodils.

That afternoon, Phil drove us to the airport. As we crossed one of Seattle's causeways, I turned to him behind the wheel next to me. "I love Nicole, Phil. Are you going to marry her some day and give me a grandchild?" The question was gentle and teasing. I had told him for years I couldn't wait to be a grandmother. His response was usually to tell me to slow down, to get off his back. He smiled. "Actually we'd love to have a child," he answered. "In fact, we were just talking about it the other night. She loves little kids as much as I do."

Settling into our seats on the plane, I turned to Angus. "Did you hear what he said about having a child? What if she's already pregnant?" My mind raced over our day and a half together. She had worn a big T-shirt for the jog. The same night for dinner she had chosen a silk blouse that hung out over a short, flippy skirt. The next morning, she wore farmer overalls. She had looked adorable. I had seen no evidence of a swollen stomach, but the more I thought about it, the more obsessed I became. They'd only been together about six weeks, much too short a time for the baby to be his. Maybe they left school and came to Seattle because of this pregnancy, to help her out. Phil would be just the one to take on a cause like this. But it was too early for that kind of responsibility; he was too young to be tied down like that. My husband thought I was crazy. He'd seen me fall into this sort of paranoid fantasizing before. By the time we reached Minneapolis, I had relented, decided to embrace this baby as my own grandchild whoever the father might be.

Over Angus's incredulous protestations, I dialed Seattle the minute we walked in the door. "Phil, I don't know any other approach with you than to be totally direct."

"What are you talking about, Mom?"

"Phil, is Nicole pregnant?"

"*What?*"

I laid it all out for him: the semester away from school, the clothes, the conversation in the car.

"Mom, you are nuts. I mean I wish in a way that it were true, but it's not. Just give it up, Mom. Forget about it."

I hung up the phone, relieved, embarrassed about my obsessive behavior, and maybe just a tiny bit disappointed that being a grandmother would have to wait.

The three of them had stayed in Seattle through the following summer, working, camping, and hiking through the neighboring mountains. They had all returned to Bates in the fall. Nicole, who was a year older than Phil, graduated in January and had gone to work in Sun Valley. Through it all—the months in school, the separation—their relationship was strong.

Nicole had been home visiting her parents in the spring, and now she had hitched a ride west with Phil on his way to Mount Rainier. Their stay with us in Minneapolis was an easy, relaxing four days. Nicole was an ultimate Frisbee player, and they played several times a day with Tia, our German shepherd, sharpening her already well-honed Frisbee skills. They took walks; they saw Phil's friends. Nicole helped me weed the vegetable garden, where she told me that she, like me, had kept a journal for years. She shared with me a quote she had written down from one of her favorite authors: "I spend most of my time inside my head." I loved that, loved her for finding it worthy of preserving.

Then one morning they packed the car full to the brim, squeezing in a box of my homemade chocolate-chip cookies. I hugged Phil tightly, then Nicole, waving them off with a full heart.

CHAPTER 7

Next of Kin

Be careful not to go up the mountain or to touch the
edge of it.

NRSV, Exodus 19:12

The August afternoon air was heavy, and a blast of heat hit me square
in the face as I reached into the oven to pull out a sheet of toasted pita
bread triangles. Only twenty minutes left until our house guests
would arrive: the first of two couples we were expecting for the weekend—Angus's Yale roommates and their wives. The three old school
chums had decided months before to converge in Minnesota; one was
flying in from Los Angeles, the other from New York. We wives—all
second marriages—were almost irrelevant to the occasion, but my
responsibility was still to provide dinner that night. The phone never
failed to ring when I could least afford the time. I parked the hot
cookie sheet and grabbed the receiver.

"Mom?"

My heart jumped and tension melted away as that warm, familiar
voice greeted my ears. Connecting with Phil had been hard all summer, ever since he had started the job at Mount Rainier Park.
Attempts to phone him were often frustrating, delayed by relay calls

from the White River Ranger Station to the tiny prefab quarters where he roomed with the head climbing ranger. I pulled the coiled wire out to its full length and settled gratefully into a nearby soft wicker armchair. The hors d'oeuvres could wait.

Phil had summited Mount Rainier the week before. The climb was hard, really hard, he said. In my mind I could see the sparkle in his eyes, the grin with a wry edge. It had been tough, he said, but he had had no trouble making it to the top. He talked on, with enthusiasm. Glacier Basin, the site where he camped and spent most of his time on the job, was so beautiful. Every day he watched deer come and drink, and often they would lie down peacefully within sight of him. On a typical day, he said, he saw more animals than people.

"Thanks again for getting Nicole's bracelet for me, Mom. It was perfect—exactly the one I remembered seeing. She loved it."

He had called me early in July and asked me to go back to the gift shop they had visited in June at the contemporary art museum, to track down a particular bracelet for her birthday. He had sent me the money, and I had been glad to oblige. The bracelet was a wide silver cuff imbedded with a smooth oval of luminous blue-green beach glass.

"Did you send it to her?"

"No, I gave it to her personally. I didn't want to tell you this, but I drove to Sun Valley for her birthday."

"You *what?*"

Nine hours there, nine hours back. I could feel the knot tightening in my stomach, the old urge to control flaring up, threatening to dampen the goodwill of this call. How could he even *think* of driving that long alone . . . so dangerous with no one to relieve him at the wheel. *But stop it*, I thought. *He's back. It's over. He's safe. We'll be together, he and I and Nicole in Seattle in just ten short days.* I had planned a trip out there to meet them and celebrate the end of both their jobs. From there they were planning to move on, to live together in Portland while he finished his last semester of school.

He had one piece of bad news. His college roommate Jeff, who was also living in Seattle, had been one of two finalists for a job with 150 applicants. He had really wanted the job, and he had lost. "He's really hurting, Mom," he said, "and I might want the money to loan him a month's rent. I don't want to do it unless I absolutely have to. I'll let you know." I was proud to hear that. I knew Phil had a big heart and would do anything for his friends, but I also loved the way he made room for Jeff's pride, wanted to wait for him to do it on his own.

"I'm going to summit again this weekend with Sean Ryan, one of the climbing rangers. I'm so psyched, Mom. It's awesome up there. I just can't wait to do it again." A prickle of fear ran up my spine. At a business dinner several nights before, I had been seated next to a man from Seattle. When I told him what my son was doing, he had shaken his head. "It's a crime," he told me, "the way these rangers have to risk their lives for so many climbers who have no business being on that mountain."

"Oh Phil, please be careful."

"Come on, Mom. I'm a good climber."

"I know you are." And I did. He was young, strong, coordinated. If anyone could do it, he could. I had been afraid so many times before, and I was used to this, to living with the fear. He always came back.

"I'll meet you at the airport a week from Monday. And whatever you do, don't worry!"

"I love you, Phil."

"I love you too, Mom."

As I hung the phone back on its wall cradle, a voice bellowed from the front door. "Who have you been talking to? We've been getting a busy signal all the way home." Angus and the first two guests had arrived. Our weekend had begun.

The weather was perfect, as August in Minnesota nearly always is, and the group got along nicely. I had met both women before, but we didn't know each other well. We had a lot in common—more than our marriages to three veterans of the Yale class of '56. We were all high-energy types, physically fit, and interested in the latest developments in women's health strategies to stay young and vital. Both of them subscribed to a women's health newsletter that they swore by, and I vowed to sign up myself. One described regular visits to have her colon flushed, a practice that I thought I might pass up, regardless of its benefits. We feasted on grilled leg of lamb, tiny potatoes from my garden, summer squash, and peaches with ice cream. The red wine flowed, and we stayed up as late as six middle-aged cronies could manage. Before bed, we stepped to the edge of the deck and looked at the nearly full moon that had painted a cool silver path toward us, sparkling on the water below. I was facing west, and I wondered, briefly, if Phil were seeing the same moon, shining over his campsite, reflecting on the pond nestled in Glacier Basin.

Saturday's weather was good on Mount Rainier. Phil's supervisor was out of town. In order to get a head start on his planned summit with Sean Ryan, he decided to play hooky, leaving his post at Glacier Basin early to hike up 5,000 feet or so to Camp Schurman. He would give himself plenty of time to acclimate to the altitude in preparation for their climb to the summit. Summit attempts are made late at night, leaving time to get to the top and return before the morning sun makes the snow too soft to traverse.

As Phil was hiking slowly upward, high above him, on the Emmons Glacier at 13,400 feet, a forty-year-old man named John Craven slipped on the hard, sheer ice and fell. His two climbing partners, a man and his daughter, leaned into the slope and dug in. The spiked crampons on their feet and the axes in their hands penetrated the ice, resisting the tremendous force tugging on the rope that bound them and their falling companion together, threatening to pull all three of them off the mountain to their deaths. The rope held. They were all safe, but Craven's ankle was badly crushed. The three of them managed to inch their way to a safer spot. While two climbers who had witnessed the fall went off to Camp Muir on the other side of the mountain to find help, the trio needing rescue hunkered down in the cold to wait.

The call came in to Camp Schurman about 5:30 that afternoon: a man was injured, and the rangers at Camp Muir were looking for a team to help with the rescue. Phil and Sean and a man named Luke Reinsma were the only ones there. Phil was essentially a volunteer. He was paid about fifty dollars a week on this summer internship, assigned to check campsites near Glacier Basin and assist hikers. Though he knew how to climb and had summited Rainier just the other day, he was far from a trained climbing ranger. Sean was a first-year ranger who had summited about twelve times, and Reinsma, a forty-seven-year-old professor, was a Seattle Mountain Rescue volunteer who had not climbed Mount Rainier since his first summit seven years earlier. The ranger in charge of the rescue, operating by radio from park headquarters, considered his options. Craven was reported to be vulnerable to shock and unable to move. He might well not survive if left all night at the top of the mountain. The team at Camp Muir, five or six hours climbing time from the injured man, was prepared to leave just after midnight. They would carry heavy evacuation gear and reach him by morning. The Schurman group, only four climbing hours away, could leave immediately, carry warm clothes, stabilize him, and stay with him until the other rescue team arrived.

The three at Camp Schurman accepted the assignment. Phil and Sean were thrilled. Phil had been yearning for this chance to join a real rescue mission. He could summit with Sean as planned and even help an injured climber in the process. The situation was too good to be true. Sean now had his chance to lead a mission, something he had never done. Reinsma, who was still recovering from double pneumonia and had not had long enough to acclimate himself to the altitude, was not so enthusiastic. The three of them gulped down a quick snack. Then they shouldered their sixty-pound packs loaded with sleeping bags, a tent, food, and fuel. At seven o'clock, roped together, they set off on the 4,000-foot climb up the Emmons Glacier, each, perhaps, assuming the others were more experienced than they were.

The going was slow, very slow. Air was thin, and they had to take a breath with every step. About an hour into the trip, as they huddled together for a break, Luke Reinsma came to grips with the fact that he couldn't proceed. He felt tired and sick from the altitude, and he knew he was slowing the progress of the two younger climbers. They learned by radio that the injured man's two companions had left him alone on the mountain. Fearing they would not all survive the night, the man and his daughter had left Craven with extra clothing and descended together to Camp Muir. This news angered Phil, and he and Sean convinced the ranger at the other end of the radio to let them go on alone. They sent Reinsma back, and, just before 9 P.M., they headed off, just the two of them together. The sky was clear, the moon was bright. They didn't even need headlamps to light their way.

Saturday had been clear and slightly cooler in the Midwest. The six of us spent a leisurely morning, then set off for a visit to the Minnesota Landscape Arboretum, a huge, sprawling complex with gardens of every description and miles of walking paths through woods and meadows. We opted for the long loop out through fields that displayed collections of every variety of tree and shrub that grow in the area. We laughed and chatted, the women walking together, leaving the three old friends to reminisce about their college days, to compare notes on their careers and their impending retirement.

Two of us barely noticed the long walk, as enthralled as we were to hear our Los Angeles companion tell us the saga of her daughter, who had been stalked by a man for months. She told us of his unrelenting phone calls, letters, and harassment, of her efforts to convince the police to stop it, of their eventual decision to move the family to a new location. How lucky I am, I thought. I couldn't imagine the havoc such an ordeal would wreak on a family.

Back home, the group prevailed on me to show them the manuscript for my master's thesis. One of my professors had suggested I try to have it published. The manuscript had just been sent back to me after spending eight months at a big West Coast publisher. Three successive editors had looked at it and considered adding it to their list of books for the upcoming season before finally rejecting it once and for all. I was feeling discouraged, depressed by the rejection and pessimistic about the book's prospects. Our friends were intrigued, and one couple asked me to let them take the manuscript home with them. That felt good. Maybe the book would find its readership one at a time.

That night, we went to a local seafood restaurant for dinner. We had managed to secure a private room for our party, and my husband and I regaled the group with tales of our new adventure in California: a field of cabernet grapevines we had just purchased for my husband's postretirement "career," fulfilling a long-held dream of his that was finally on the verge of coming true. Over bowls of steaming mussels and plates of blackened swordfish, they helped us dream up names for the new vineyard: Terra Springs, Oak Hill. . . . One roommate told us he would donate his legal skills to register the names in California just in case. Back home, we fell asleep exhausted. I never gave even a passing thought to Mount Rainier.

As Saturday night wore on, the weather had changed on the mountain. The temperature had dropped below zero and the wind raged. A group of climbers passed Sean and Phil on the way down, telling them the conditions were too risky, that they had made the decision to turn around. About 11:30 A.M., Sean Ryan radioed the ranger station. He could hardly be heard over the howling wind. Gasping for breath, Sean said they had made it to 12,900 feet. The going was slow, but they could see the area where the injured climber waited above them. They had been having trouble though, he added. Phil's ill-fitting crampon had broken, and they had been attempting to fix it. They were determined to keep going. The ranger wished them well, and Ryan signed off.

What happened next will forever be shrouded in mystery. Sometime shortly after that radio call, one of them fell. Perhaps Phil, stopping to adjust his broken crampon, slipped on the sheet of ice that covered the mountain. Perhaps Sean, later found with one glove off, had reached back to put his radio in his pack and was caught off balance, blown off the slope by the gale-force winds. The rope that bound them together made them one, for better or for worse, and within seconds they were both sliding, out of control, to their deaths on the glacier 1,200 feet below.

The rangers working the radios tried without success all night long to contact Sean and Phil. At around seven the next morning, the team from Camp Muir reached John Craven, who had survived the night. His ankle was in pain, but he was otherwise stable. When they realized Sean and Phil had never arrived, the Park Service turned its attention to the lost young rangers. At nine-thirty Sunday morning, after being dispatched to the rescue to deliver Craven to a waiting ambulance, a Chinook helicopter returned to the Emmons Glacier and hovered there, looking for Sean and Phil. At last they were spotted, lying surrounded by blocks of ice, snow drifting over their still bodies, joined together by their climbing rope. At 1:30 Sunday afternoon, they were loaded into the helicopter and flown away. For reasons we still don't understand, twenty-four hours would pass before the Park Service could find and inform the next of kin.

CHAPTER 8

House of Prayer

One thing I feared, and it befell, and what I dreaded
came to me.

Job 3:25, translated by Raymond P. Scheindlin

Sunday morning we pulled our deck table into the shade under a
spreading oak tree. We covered the table with a bright country
French tablecloth and set out our favorite yellow and blue Italian
pottery. Angus cooked up an omelet loaded with fresh vegetables
from the garden. We toasted English muffins, spread them lavishly
with raspberry jam from the local farmer stand, and washed it all
down with fresh-squeezed orange juice and coffee. Can this possibly
be the Minnesota they had heard about, our friends teased? The land
of ice and snow? Why go back home either east or west when
Shangri-La was right here in the heartland?

Our friends from New York left for the airport around noon, and
the remaining four of us took a bike ride for an hour or so. We pedaled leisurely along abandoned railroad beds that have been made into
miles of suburban bicycle paths, winding around marshes throbbing
with birdsong, glowing with purple loosestrife.

After the last guests left, I packed a bag and loaded my bike on the back of the car, bound for the Episcopal House of Prayer near St. John's University, about an hour northeast of the Twin Cities. I was a board member of this retreat house, which had been founded by my mentor, the bishop. I had signed up for a weeklong retreat where Marcus Borg, a renowned Jesus scholar, would be in residence. Angus left for a business trip to Chicago.

As I drove, I thought about my father. A survivor of two bouts with cancer, he had just spent a few days in the hospital, grappling with complications from some of the earlier surgery. Not knowing whether he was truly out of the woods, I hated to leave for a week, concerned that perhaps the scar tissue would cause a blockage again, leading to another hospital stay. I wanted to be close by to support him.

I arrived at the House of Prayer, a lovely wood and fieldstone building, nestled in the woods on the grounds of nearby St. John's Benedictine abbey. I settled into my room—a tiny, simple cubicle with a tall narrow window that opened to the wildness of the surrounding woods. I drew a slow, deep breath. I had a slight nagging stomachache. Perhaps it was worry over my Dad, I thought. I was tired, and I needed this peace and quiet, this time apart from my hectic life. Being here was good.

Marcus Borg was a friendly, bearded man with a twinkle in his eye. He joined the twenty or so retreatants for a casual dinner on Sunday night, then conducted the first session that evening. He challenged us to think back on our earliest images and impressions of Jesus, and we broke up into small groups to compare our stories.

I woke very early Monday morning, heading out the door just at dawn for a short walk along the road among the fields and farmhouses that surround the House of Prayer. As I walked along, I saw far up ahead of me in the dim light something lying on the road. I approached and made out an exquisite fox. Its perfect tail was spread out, its lovely body lying there, staring through hollow eyes. The fox was not a baby, but young, with no sign of injury on its body. I kept walking, but I couldn't push the fox out of my mind. How could I leave that beautiful creature there for another car to run over? I am normally afraid of dead animals and repulsed by the thought of touching them, but I turned and walked back to the fox. I ran my hand along the full length of its body, feeling the softness of its fur all the way to the tip of its lush, full tail. I hesitated, pushing down the fear, then lifted it gently off the road. I laid it down under a tree, fluffing a patch of grass on which I gently placed its head.

Before we began the day's first lecture, we gathered for a half-hour meditation session, which was nothing new for me. I had had a meditation practice for nearly four years, sitting in silence for about twenty minutes each morning at home. I sat in a chair instead of my usual cushion on the floor, and I went into myself, into the silence. Suddenly my lower spine and my intestines began to contract, to gather in, a paroxysm of anxiety that I couldn't explain. My stomach, which had been bothering me constantly since the night before, hardened into a tight, painful ball. I felt a hot wave rise from my lower gut and spread slowly up my body, radiating out into every limb, into every pore. My breathing became short and tight, and I could feel my skin dampen. Somehow, through sheer endurance practice, I stuck it out through the half hour, but when the time was over, I went up to David Keller, the House of Prayer's director, a friend and trusted spiritual mentor. I told him about my experience and asked if he had ever had such a thing happen. He looked concerned. He said he had occasionally felt a sensation of warmth spreading over him that he thought might be a sign of the presence of God, "but this doesn't sound like that," he said. I left the encounter confused, wondering if it could possibly be a first menopausal hot flash, and feeling exposed, raw, and dissatisfied with the explanation.

After the morning lecture and lunch, the afternoon was free. Several of us left to visit a neighboring town to look at a sculpture exhibition. Nell, a fellow board member of the House of Prayer, was a relatively new friend. More than fifteen years my senior, a native of

South Carolina, she was a talented painter, a tireless worker for social causes. She had audited a graduate course I had recently taken on the letters of Paul, along with her friend Van, who was with her that day too. I admired Nell, whose energy and enthusiasms mirrored my own. We three women and another, an Episcopal priest, rode bicycles we had brought along. Two male companions were on roller blades. One of them was my old friend Howard, a newly ordained Episcopal priest who lived near the northern border of Minnesota. Howard was energy-filled, bright-eyed, and warm. I had hardly seen him since he had been assigned to his new church up north. I adored him and felt so lucky that we had both turned up at this conference, that we had time together at last. The day was sunny and cooler, and the outing was just what we all needed.

We arrived back at the House of Prayer about five, flushed with fresh air and exercise. As I pedaled down the gravel driveway, a fellow retreatant waiting there waved me inside, saying that David Keller had an important message for me. I stopped, hesitated, then headed toward his office. I was afraid something had happened to my father. I rounded the corner.

"It's about my dad, isn't it?"

"No," he said. He took hold of my shoulders, gently, firmly. He took a deep breath, then looked directly into my eyes. "Margaret, Phil was killed in a climbing accident." I took in that serene face, those honest blue eyes, saw his lips forming that message. I looked hard at him, trying to understand the words. I stepped back and thumped his chest with my fists.

"You're joking," I said. I felt my lips beginning to tremble, heard my voice crack. "Tell me it isn't true."

"It is true," he said.

As I stared, he repeated the words slowly two more times. "Your son Phil was killed. He died yesterday in a climbing accident on Mount Rainier."

My blood and the bile in my stomach hardened to cement, and I dropped to the floor from the weight of it. I stayed there, my arms and hands spread out, needing the security of the ground. Sounds I had never heard before rose from my throat. Nausea pressed up at the base of my jaw. I was hot, then freezing cold. I kept thinking that I had known this would happen. All the hours of fear, all those years of worry had come true. My mind raced like a film on fast forward. How had it happened? I had no more children. Did Angus know? Now I knew when and how he would die. Phil *had* died. He was actually gone. I had no son. I had no other children. I would never have grand-children. I would never see him again, not ever, ever again. It wasn't true. It was a horrible dream. New thoughts piled on each other like an avalanche threatening to bury me. I pounded the floor, curled in a ball, scratched at the carpet. I felt arms reaching out to me, hands stroking me, but no one could touch me.

CHAPTER 9

Echoes

Let tears run down like a river day and night; give thy-
self no rest; let not the apple of thine eye cease.
Lamentations 2:18 KJV

They took me over to David's house, where I was to receive a call
from Angus, whom they had reached in Chicago, and from my parents. I sat in David's living room with its comfortable furniture, its
view out into the surrounding woods. I sat holding my stomach, feeling as if I had swallowed bags of cotton. I rocked and wailed. I waited
there on the couch, curled in a ball. I was furious, then desperate, then
betrayed. My head hurt. My nose ran, and my sinuses were so full that
my ears were exploding from the pressure. *Why? Why me?* My teeth
chattered. I felt so lonely. I had lost my best friend. There would be
no wedding, no grandchildren. But where was Phil? I wanted to hold
him, to comfort him. I was no longer a mother. My life was over.

Nell came and sat beside me, held me like a baby, and I let myself
dissolve, sobbing in her lap. They gave me water and love, and they
listened to me. "God is punishing me," I said. "My life has been too
good, too perfect. I knew it couldn't last."

I tried to stand up from the couch, and my hips were completely numb. No connection existed between my brain and my legs. I couldn't make my legs move. I was afraid I would never walk again. Nell and David held me up between them, made me walk down the driveway until the feeling gradually came back. I told them then how complete I felt with Phil. I remembered our final phone call, how the last words we said to each other were that we loved each other. I thought about how I loved him, a visceral, animal kind of love. I told them I would never love like that again. Then the moans, unstoppable—like the urge to push during childbirth—would rise again, and I would let them come, giving voice to the hopelessness, the incredible permanence of it all. No empty spaces were present between my son and me, no regrets. "At some level I have always known this would happen," I kept repeating. "It's just that now I know when and how."

At last the phone rang. It was Angus. The agreed-upon time to call me had come, and he was on an airplane, flying home from Chicago. As I gave vent to my feelings, there he sat, wedged between strangers thirty thousand feet in the air, fighting back tears, unable to talk above a whisper. My heart broke for him too, losing this stepson he had lived with for eighteen years, whom I knew he loved deeply. "I'll see you at home in an hour or so," he said.

"Drive carefully," I added in a desperate afterthought.

Someone had packed my bag and loaded it along with my bike into the back of my car. Howard, the priest who had been biking with us, drove. Nell rode along in the back seat. David's wife followed us so she could drive them back again.

Howard reached over and grabbed my shoulder. "I want to tell you a story," he said, as we drove past acres of cornfields, the windshield devouring the monotonous gray path before us. "I almost died once, and I need to tell you about it." He had been surfing, somewhere in Hawaii where he once lived. A huge wave knocked him down. He swam with all his might, but he was going in the wrong direction, and he hit bottom. He pushed off, hard, and just as he came up, another wave came and knocked him down. He blacked out, and then, in a way, died. He said he felt as if he was moving down a long, dark tunnel, and as he approached the end, a huge white light began to glow, like nothing he'd ever experienced. He washed up on the beach, and someone revived him. "But you know," he said, looking intently at me, "I was depressed for weeks, because I wanted to go back to that warm, wonderful place of light." I believed him, and I felt better for a minute or two. Whatever the aftermath might be of this huge wave that had just knocked me down and washed me up on the shore, I knew that the pain, the grief, the panic I felt were for *me*, not Phil. I knew somehow that he was safe, that he was beyond danger for the first time. At least the *fear* for him is gone forever, I thought. He is fine, wherever, whatever he is.

As we descended our steep driveway, I could see my parents step out of their car and start toward our house. They looked small, vulnerable, and suddenly old. For years, my mother's attempts to mother me had been annoying. I wanted to be a friend, a peer, nothing more. Now I ran into her arms and buried my face in her shoulder. I saw that this fragile body, smaller now than mine, was still the anchor of my life, could still offer a measure of comfort against the worst pain I had ever known. I turned to my father, just recovering from a hospital stay himself, just then knowing that his namesake, his first grandchild, was dead. I could see the deepened lines on his face, see that life—however much he had cherished it, however it had motivated him to fight off these physical threats he had fiercely overcome—had suddenly lost its luster. "Why him?" he said. "It should have been me." I held him, let him hold me tight, and I knew that buried in all the waves of grief was relief that he was still there with me, that I would never, could never have asked for such a trade.

Then I heard the crunch of gravel, a car coming down the driveway. There was Angus. As we held each other, as I felt my last bit of strength ebbing away, I knew that this love I felt for him, this core, this nucleus into which everything else dissolved, was where the rest of my life—if there was one—would have to begin.

Angus and I were alone with my parents. We had climbed into a stage set. The second-story living room in what was our home, the airy house we built together, where we had spent every summer of the last fifteen years, now felt foreign, strange. The furniture was the same, but I didn't recognize it. The reds and yellows of the colorful fabrics were pale, inert. A chill settled in the room, even though the sun was shining, and the air outside was hot and muggy. I watched the green leaves tossing on the branches of the trees outside the windows, glinting in the sunlight. They were mocking me, staking out a border between the world out *there*—where everything was normal, where everything was as it had always been—and in *here*, in this nightmare world I didn't know and didn't want to be part of.

Maybe from force of habit, maybe because we were desperate for something to do, Angus and I wandered back to our bedroom and pushed the button on the telephone answering machine. The first message was from Chris, my thirty-one-year-old stepson, calling from his home in Boulder. A friend of his from Seattle had just called him, saying he had heard on the news that a young man from Minnesota had been killed on Mount Rainier. They weren't releasing any names. Chris was worried. Could it possibly be Phil? Hearing the love and panic in Chris's voice reminded me that I had three stepchildren. In my shock and grief, I had focused only on myself, on my own pain, on the fact that I had given birth to only one child. Now I remembered. Now we would have to be the bearers of bad news. We would have to tell them, to shatter their worlds as ours had been shattered. Knowing that three others would soon share our grief offered a kind of comfort. "Not yet," Angus said. "I can't bear to call them all quite yet."

We pushed the button on the phone again and heard a faint,

trembling voice. It was Nicole, who had called from Sun Valley, hours earlier. I stopped the machine, grabbed the receiver, and dialed.

"Nicole?"

At the sound of my voice, she erupted into sobs, and I too dissolved again. For minutes—five? ten?—we cried half a continent apart. We had both felt the wedge of a giant axe cleave our lives in two. For both of us, life as we had known it was over, utterly destroyed. Nicole had quit her job just days before. She had nearly finished packing her things and loading them into her car. In just over a week she would have joined Phil and me in Seattle, and now her entire life hung there, empty, without anchor, mired in grief. "I didn't know what to do except go out and run," she said. "There are lupine growing along the river here, and I have been picking them, bringing them home. They're like the ones on Mount Rainier."

We agreed that she would wait there in Sun Valley for Jeff, their former roommate, who was already on his way, driving from Seattle. Then the two of them would fly to Minneapolis to be with us.

A knock at the door. I see a sallow young man come up the stairs, a stranger, a macabre figure dressed in a uniform. He asks for me. He is pale and frightened. He is shaking in his stiffness. His duty, he says, is to inform me that my son, Philip James Otis, an employee of the National Park Service, is dead. He was killed night before last in a rescue attempt on Mount Rainier. I think, It is like a war. I am every mother who has confronted a stranger like this one.

One by one, our dearest friends gathered in the living room. They came in couples, alone, however they happened to be when they heard the news. Almost no conversation took place, only silence, shock. No one tried to make us feel better, because nothing would have worked. We simply sat together, felt together, and watched the hands of the clock turn slowly. I wanted only one thing: to turn that clock around, to see it wind backwards, to think of a way to stop the world and go back to Saturday afternoon, to do something, anything to make it all come out differently.

I heard the screen door slam, and my old friend Nancy was on the stairs. She, like many of the others, had driven half an hour to our house to be there after hearing the news. Just four days before, we had celebrated her fiftieth birthday. Her friends had thrown a big party, because the week before that, the last week of her forties, she had learned she had ovarian cancer. I had listened to her then, supported her, agonized with her at the unfairness of it all. Now she was here to comfort me. We looked at each other. After thirty-five years of friendship, how could these two earthshaking, life-transforming events have happened to us both, within a week? What convergence was this—in the season in which we would both celebrate our fiftieth birthdays— that at its midpoint life would utterly turn on us? We held each other in disbelief.

I lay in bed listening to Angus call his children, my stepchildren. With each one, I braced myself as I waited to hear him pronounce, "Phil has been killed." The horrible words penetrated, each time, like a knife. I pictured Chris, then Andrew, then Heidi in turn. I knew their sudden stomachaches, the pressure behind their eyes, the welling pain. I ached for them, hearing this news all alone in Colorado, in California. I wanted them home with us. I felt protective, anxious, like a mother would. I remembered then that I loved them.

The night came. I turned; I rolled over. No position was comfortable. I passed the hours on top of a cold, icy mountain. I watched my son slip, fall, tumble through space, again and again. I tried to enter his mind, to know if he knew he was dying. I wanted to know if he thought of me, of his family, or of Nicole as he was falling. I wondered if he had felt the pain. I imagined what it would be like to be dead. I wondered if he still had thoughts and feelings, if he knew he had died, if he knew how empty and sad I was. The night was interminable. At last the horizon began to gray. A faint light swelled over the marsh. A goose took flight, and its cries—long, mournful honks—took me back to the mountain. Did he cry as he fell? Was there a wail? Did anyone hear it? Did it echo endlessly, bounce from one peak to another, rise to disappear in the howl of the wind?

Camp Phil

God places these souls in the dark night so as to purify
them of their imperfections and make them advance.

John of the Cross

"We need to walk," Angus pronounced. "We have to move, to stay
active." Even though he is eleven years my senior, Angus had been
physically out ahead of me all the eighteen years of our married life,
goading me, always, into yet another walk, an afternoon ski, into
more activity than I had energy. I had usually resisted, then been
grateful for the push. This morning was no exception.

My teeth chattering, I slowly pulled on a pair of shorts, a T-shirt,
and my shoes. Emerging tentatively into the humid morning air, we
were astronauts stepping out onto a new planet. I was stooped, bent
with the pain in my stomach. I was dizzy, my inner ears pressed by
swollen sinuses. My eyes were stinging, raw, singed from the relentless salt. I hung from Angus's right arm with both my hands. I shuffled
along next to him, one step at a time, praying we would not encounter
any of the neighbors. We slowly navigated the mile-long loop that
threads through our neighborhood. When we finally descended our
driveway again, the sun was just peeking up over the marsh.

On our front walk stood Jane and Walter Barry, old friends and next-door neighbors, grocery bags in their arms. Their son Stew was one of Phil's best friends, and they must have heard the news overnight. There they were, even Jane, who is slow to rise in the morning, who loves to linger over coffee in her robe. The morning had just dawned, and they had already trekked to the store for fresh orange juice, rolls, and fruit. Now they were delivering it to our door. I was flooded with gratitude, with the sudden knowledge that—though we seemed to be alone, singled out by this tragedy—other lives were interrupted too, and others shared our pain. They wondered what they could do to help us, what role they might play as neighbors. Together we came to the thought that young people might be arriving in the next few days. Perhaps they could help look after them in some way. We said our good-byes, and as they headed out the door, Jane stopped. She turned her streaked face back, looked up toward me. "I'll share Stew with you," she offered.

My ex-husband Todd was the first one to call that morning. In the horrendous hours of the previous day and night, my thoughts had turned often to Todd. The day before, he had been found home first by the uniformed messenger. Todd had tried to find me, then called my mother and told her the news. If this was unbearable for me, I thought, it would have to be even worse for him. My mind kept coming back to the feeling that I was so complete with Phil, that I had no major regrets, that we had no empty places between us, which gave me some solace in the midst of the anguish. I knew that for Todd, who had left our marriage and left us both shortly after Phil's first birthday, there might be some regrets.

Since our divorce, as the pain and hurt subsided, as we both settled into separate marriages and separate lives, Todd and I had worked out a cordial relationship. I had full custody of Phil, but we cooperated well. When Phil was small, we would compare notes each weekend to see which couple had plans which night. Then Phil would spend the night with whichever couple was home. When I traveled, either for short business trips or long vacations, Phil would live with Todd and his wife and two daughters. For years, Phil nearly avoided babysitters altogether. Todd had sometimes joined us for teacher conferences. But for the most part, the major decisions—the schools, the summer plans, the lessons, the disciplining—had been mine and Angus's.

Todd had seen Phil, though, more recently than we had. He and his daughter Madeline had traveled to Mount Rainier just a few weeks before. They had gone hiking together, backpacking, and Phil had been cheery and supportive, encouraging Madeline, who struggled with asthma in the altitude. Now Todd was on the other end of the telephone line, his voice breaking, his pain as unbearable as mine. He had left so many decisions to me in Phil's short life. Now we had a funeral to plan. He needed to be with us. He would be there within the hour.

I was sitting outside on the deck. My mother had come. She had taken over the kitchen, answering the phone, writing down messages. She kept track of everything—flowers, food, calls—on yellow pads. I was useless, freezing cold in the ninety-degree heat, shivering. I kept trying to picture Phil's body. Where was it? Who was taking care of it? I wanted to see him, to be with him. I knew he was dead, that nothing more could be done. I knew he was dead when they found him, but I kept imagining that he was looking for me, lying somewhere all alone, wondering where his mother was. How could I leave him to strangers, lying in a cold, dark room on a table somewhere near Mount Rainier? But how could I go there, when I couldn't even make it to the bathroom without help?

I heard Todd's car in the driveway. I stood up, every muscle aching, and went slowly down to greet him. He was pale and tired, and his thin lips were drawn down with tension and pain. We held each other for a minute or so, but the contact offered no relief. I had been wondering whether the death of our son might suddenly erase nearly two decades of estrangement, whether I might be drawn to him once again, but seeing his agony only seemed to intensify my own.

Angus and Todd went inside together to telephone the Tacoma medical examiner, to dial a number that the uniformed young man had given us the night before. I settled back into my chair on the deck.

He confirmed that Phil's body was there and said they had already completed the autopsy requested by the Park Service. Angus had asked them whether we should travel to Washington. "He's pretty banged up," they had said. "We don't really recommend you come to see the body." *Pretty banged up* . . . what did that mean? I tried to picture Phil's broken body, to see his face again, to imagine what it would look like with the life drained out of it. But I was too weak to protest, too stunned to move, in too much shock to do anything except sit there inside the ice shield that was forming around my own body that had me frozen to the chair. It would take a week or ten days, they said, to get his body released, to send it home.

Our family had always believed in cremation, which perhaps went along with a secular orientation, or perhaps it was just modern. The body is no longer the person, I had always been told. I heard them saying this now from under the ice, as if I were hearing it with someone else's ears. *This isn't just a body. This is my son.* A decision was made, right there in front of me, to have him cremated in Washington, to have his ashes flown home several days later. I acquiesced; I could do nothing more.

So this is how it ends: that dear body, flesh of my flesh. I thought back to a warm, sunny day in high spring: May 24, 1973, the day of Phil's birth.

As we left for the hospital around noon, I posed for a picture in front of the lilac bush by our porch, my body bursting like the dangling purple clusters of blossom that wafted their perfumed essence over my head like a blessing. Labor took sixteen hours from start to finish, from the first tentative squeeze next to my heart in the half-light before dawn until I heard the words, "You have a son!" four minutes after ten that night. I was tired. I had reupholstered four pieces of porch furniture in a burst of energy the day before. In giving birth, I had turned myself inside out like a snake shedding a full length of skin. I drifted off to sleep that night, grateful and as happy as I ever hoped to be again.

The next morning, the nurse handed me my robust, red-faced, screaming son, wrapped tight as a cabbage roll in a thin flannel blanket. I unwrapped him carefully like a Christmas present, examining every inch of that newly minted body, from the round, misshapen head to the squirming fingers and toes. I watched his tiny mouth earnestly root, felt the sharp sting of suction at my nipple, then relief as the engorged hardness of my breast slowly gave itself up to his hunger, becoming soft and empty again. I watched the tiny hand search, grope, scratch, the delicate razor-sharp corners of his nails catching on my nightgown. The miniature fist found my finger, closed around it with astounding strength. I leaned down. My lips grazed lightly along the soft down on his head, traced the lumps and bumps on his just-born skull. To the sound of gentle gulping, I breathed in, savoring a delicate scent imperceptible from even six inches away, but up close a delectable perfumed blend of baby powder, honey, and yogurt that entered me and stimulated a response of love and possessiveness I had never known. This cuddly creature, the undeniable heft of him in my arms, declared its presence, overwhelmed me with messages.

By contrast, the death of my son was pure hearsay. I understood what had happened, but I was swallowed into an impenetrable fog of disbelief. I had not seen, touched, or smelled any evidence of his death. I wanted to run to his side, to hold him. I needed to see for myself that he was dead. I wanted to prove that it was not true, that it was all just a nightmare.

I knew, as I sat there on the deck, as the hours of the morning dragged on, that we would have to start thinking about a memorial service for Phil. A memorial service is what one did at times like this, wasn't it? Even the thought of a service made his death so real somehow, so final. How amazing, I thought, that we would know just where to turn, how to go about such a daunting prospect. Five years before, we would have been swimming in confusion, without direction or guidance, with nowhere to go.

Now, here we were, flattened by Phil's death. Instead of being adrift in our secular world, we had a church; we were grounded in the liturgy of the *Book of Common Prayer*; and we had a veritable network of clergy to support us. In the hours since I had learned of Phil's death, the serendipity of it all had occurred to me. Suddenly the whole process I had been through seemed like a preparation for this moment.

In my tossing and turning the night before, I thought a lot about God, about this new underlying presence in my life that I had come to trust, to count on, to look to for guidance. Until now, God had seemed to be a positive force, a source of support, a deep, mysterious well into which I could dip when my spirit was thirsty. I had learned to open myself inward, leading ultimately beyond myself, to receive direction from the resonant stillness inside of me. Now I froze. I did not know which way to turn. What was this new sadistic twist in my story? Was Phil's death my reward for conversion, this pain the consequence of joining the church? What had gone wrong? Was I suddenly being confronted with a punishing, vengeful God, one I had never acknowledged? In my late-night agony, I curled up in a ball, wanting to hide from the darkness that engulfed me.

But another voice argued inside of me overnight, one that reminded me that we are free agents, that Phil had chosen to climb, to become an intern on Mount Rainier. My God was not a micromanager, prone to selective murder. Weather can be fierce; accidents happen. Phil led a life full of risk, on the edge. Perhaps I had discovered God just in time. Was it not amazing that I had this new support system, this new vocabulary to help me wrestle with what fate had dealt me?

The phone rang. My mother came out to tell me it was Jean Vail, the interim dean of St. Mark's Cathedral, the one to whom we would now need to turn to guide us through the process of planning a memorial service.

Three years before, when I was in the midst of my spiritual awakening, Angus and I had been in Chicago for a weekend, on a business trip for him. I was eager to sample a new church, so Sunday morning we wandered over for the early service in the chapel at St. James Cathedral, near our hotel. A woman was presiding at the service, and later, when it was over—as we walked back up Michigan Avenue—I began to cry. The day was beautiful and sunny, and nothing in particular was wrong with my life.

"Why are you crying?" Angus asked, looking at me, mystified.

"I don't know." I thought hard as we walked. "There was something about that woman, that priest. She moved me. I don't get it. It just makes me sad."

We went back to our hotel room, where I happened to have my laptop computer with me for a class I was taking. I opened a document and labeled it "Jean Parker Vail." I tried to write about what I was feeling, but the writing went nowhere. Perhaps, I thought, it was simply that she manifested the female presence of God. But I couldn't explain the tears, couldn't name the powerful movement I felt in my soul. Within weeks, I had moved the file to the electronic trash and emptied it.

Months later—more than a year before this day—Angus and I had been sitting at St. Mark's on a Sunday morning. Someone stood up to announce the name of the new interim dean whom the search committee had just selected. It was Jean Parker Vail from Chicago. My heart skipped.

She assumed her new job several weeks later. I introduced myself and invited her out to lunch almost immediately. Over vegetable soup at a nearby café, I told her why I had called her so urgently. She is a handsome, distinguished, gray-haired woman, who had been educated, like me, at an eastern women's college. About ten years older than I, she had stayed home with her children in the tradition of her generation. Then, at midlife, she had gone to seminary and been ordained a priest in the Episcopal church. She was a balanced blend—in the Anglican tradition—of the intellectual and the intuitive, of clear thinking and natural, empathetic compassion.

She teared up immediately when she heard my story of our encounter in Chicago, and she told me she'd have to look up the sermon she had given that day. "No," I said, "it wasn't the sermon. I'm sure of that." For months—as our friendship had deepened—I had been searching, waiting for the mystery to be revealed. Now, hearing her name, I figured it out at last. Of course. I couldn't help crying that day in Chicago, because the woman I had just seen would be presiding at my own son's memorial service three years later. I ran to the phone and grabbed it like a lifeline.

We were driving to the airport to pick up the kids—Chris from Boulder, and Andrew and Heidi from San Francisco. I was worried. How was I going to feel when I saw my stepchildren? A place inside of me was keeping score. Angus had three; I had one. How could life be so cruel? What had I done to deserve this, and why should he, who already had such an abundance of children, get off scot-free? I stole a look at him driving next to me. I saw the tense set of his jaw, the stoop of his shoulders, and I knew, of course, that he wasn't free at all, that he was suffering too, just like me. But how would I feel about *them*? I wondered. Would I resent their presence, their very aliveness? Would I forever compare them to Phil, find them lacking?

Angus left me briefly in the terminal to find out the gates of the flights we were meeting. I sat alone, afraid, in a bank of chairs. Suddenly, I felt a gentle hand on my shoulder. I looked up. It was Chris. He had arrived a few minutes early and had been looking for us. He hugged me. He was tall and strong. I could see the pain on his face. I knew he loved Phil, and that love was a bond between us. I felt safe, supported.

The three of us stood waiting at the gate, watching the passengers on the four o'clock flight from San Francisco file off the plane. My throat was constricted with the effort to keep myself from crying, here in this public place. Suddenly I saw Heidi at the door of the ramp. She was not the lithe, blond young woman I knew, not the smiling, stylish twenty-seven-year-old I was beginning to relate to as an adult friend. She moved as if the weight of centuries was on her shoulders; her face was contorted as she surveyed the crowd, tears were streaming down her cheeks. Andrew was right behind her, tears in his eyes, telling me he was so sad, he missed Phil so much. As I hugged them each in turn, I knew that I would not resent my stepchildren; rather, they would be my salvation. This was my family. I knew then that there *would* be weddings; there *would* be grandchildren. My life was not over. These children might not be my flesh and blood, but we loved each other, and I could hold on to that.

When we arrived home, the house was alive. I had nearly forgotten I had a business, that work needed to be done. Just a year or so earlier, three partners and I founded a small book-publishing venture called Hungry Mind Press. I had been working hard that summer, participating in editorial decisions and overseeing the covers and other aspects of production. Now here was Gail, one of my partners, bustling around our living room, having taken over the command post from my mother. She showed us pages of notes and telephone calls on the yellow pad. Flowers were filling every tabletop, every corner of the living room. Food was piled on the kitchen counters. I admired a huge bouquet from friends whose own daughter had been killed years before. "We understand," said the card. Just that. A perfect, single rose was delivered by another friend, from her own garden.

I lingered over an empty bird nest, a gift from a young man who often helped me in my garden, whose own mother had died a couple of years before. I stared at the nest, and I remembered a dream, an August night almost exactly a year before: *I am standing in a room on an upper floor. Outside an open window is a tree, and in the tree is a bird's nest filled with baby birds of varying sizes. Someone who is with me tells me that these birds must not enter our space, must not come in through the open window, or they will die. One by one, out of our control, they begin to leave the nest, to fly. First a big one, then a tiny miniature one: they fly away, then they turn toward us. They fly toward the open window, and I wake up, knowing that they will die.*

I looked at Gail. Suddenly I was stung by the thought of all that needed doing at our tiny, understaffed office. She read my mind. "Don't even *think* about the press," she said firmly, preparing to go home to her own house. "We'll manage just fine. When the time comes, you can do whatever you *want* to do. Now, just leave everything to us." I breathed gratefully into that space, into the relief that afforded.

Angus and I fell into bed, utterly exhausted. We had had nothing to eat for a day and a half. I swallowed a sleeping pill, prescribed over the phone by the same doctor who had brought Phil into the world. At last I closed my eyes and passed into a deep, dreamless sleep.

At four o'clock the next morning, I lay there, awake, thinking about John of the Cross. I remembered how in my studies I had puzzled long over this intense Spanish monk, how I had tried to imagine sitting with him for spiritual direction. Now, he was seemingly here again, in this predawn light, confronting me one more time. I had been pushing against him so long that I had tired of the battle.

I remembered how I had faced him down before when I was in the first throes of new spiritual growth. I had told him that I had not lost touch with the world of the senses, that I never would. I loved good food too much, reveled in music, in sensual pleasures. I had stubbornly warned him off, told him he was wrong, that not everyone who aspired to spiritual progress would have to take his arduous path, to suffer his dark nights.

Now, as I lay in bed, I was aware that a new world surrounded me—an alien, threatening place. I used to see clearly; things were outlined, etched in light and shadow, painted in brilliant color. Everything now had gone out of focus. The universe had turned gray, as if I were looking through smoked glass. I had no interest in food. Joy was a forgotten concept, one I doubted I should ever see again. I had no energy, no positive life force. *Yes*, I thought reluctantly; *I see now*. I acknowledged at last with deference this John of the Cross, this ancient presence that lurked in my room. *Yes, I see now*.

My mother and Gail, in answering the phone the day before, had held our friends off a bit, told them that Wednesday afternoon, from three to five, would be a good time for visitors. Now that time was upon us. People came alone, in groups, bearing food and flowers. They surrounded us all with love and concern. I had dressed in clean clothes, even taken a shower and combed my hair. I watched myself from a distance. I separated from my body, let my persona rise to the surface. I became a social being again, gracious, strong. I shed few tears, mustered occasional grateful smiles.

The family pulled up chairs around the dining-room table and managed to force down a couple bites of food. Nothing tasted good. I had no desire to eat. We heard a car door slam in the driveway. Then on the stairs, like a ghost, stood Nicole. She was pale, exhausted. Her hair had been dyed jet-black. I remembered then that Phil had told me about her hair experiment, that he hadn't liked it when he went to see her in Sun Valley, that he had let her know how he felt. Jeff, Phil's college roommate, was with her. He had left Seattle in a daze, driving immediately off to Sun Valley as soon as he had heard the news. They had flown in half an hour or so ago, and someone had met them at the airport. Jeff had nothing with him except the clothes on his back.

Now Nicole burst into tears, ran into my arms. I held her, stroking her back, but I could not cry. My eyes felt parched and dry; my face was impenetrable. I was a clay statue with a cracked surface, one that had been fired into an iron shell. I thought about how unfeeling I must seem to her, a petrified mother with a heart of stone. I looked at her, my lips trembling. "I don't know what has happened to me," I said. "I can't seem to cry any more."

As Angus and I stood there in the living room talking with Nicole and Jeff, I could hear more car doors slam, hear voices drifting up from the driveway. Soon, young people began filing up the stairs, one after another. There was tall, lanky Dryw, Phil's soul mate from high school, the one he had bicycled with from Minnesota to California during senior year. There was Stew Barry, just home from New York. He was big and strong, but soft around the edges, like a wonderful teddy bear. Other high school classmates arrived, male and female, all friends.

As the evening wore on, more groups of young men and women arrived—friends from Bates. There were Pete, Ben, Shane, Dave, all of whom we had met at Parents' Weekends; still others came whom we didn't know. There were rugby teammates, even the rugby coach.

They had flown in from Maine, from Connecticut, from Montana. Someone had known their flights, met them at the airport. Cars arrived with New York license plates, rental cars, a Jeep from Kansas City. How had they heard about Phil's death? How had they found us, learned their way to our house? Suddenly our living room was full. I was overwhelmed. What could we possibly do with them all? They loved Phil; they were here to be with us. Where would they sleep? What would they eat? I began to panic, to ask these questions out loud.

"Not to worry, Mrs. Wurtele," someone said. "We're all staying at Camp Phil."

What on earth was Camp Phil? I looked around, confused. Then, little by little, they filled us in. The Barrys, after they left us the other morning, had turned their entire house next door inside out. They had had a huge vinyl banner made and hung it from the trees in the backyard, mounted another metal sign out front. In white letters on a green background, they read "CAMP PHIL." Tents, borrowed from other neighbors, were pitched all over the yard. There was soda and beer in coolers, food spread out on tables. A video player was running all the time, playing old tapes of Phil that people had found. Piles of photographs were available, and Jane had bought a special book and laid it out on a table with pens nearby, a place for people to write letters to Phil.

I sat down, dazed, on the couch. I looked at Dryw, who sat down next to me, serious, stunned, like a robot. His face was so familiar, his lean frame a stake against the wind. He knew Phil, loved him. They had spent hours, days, weeks together. I found comfort in his nearness, as if a little bit of Phil still clung to him.

CHAPTER 11

We Make Our Song

Down, down, down into the darkness of the grave
Gently they go, the beautiful, the tender, the kind.

Edna St. Vincent Millay

I was tortured, at night and even in my waking hours, by images playing and replaying in my imagination. In these scenes, I was huddled
against the wind and cold on a mountain slope covered with a thick
coat of ice. As I watched, immobile, frozen in place, Phil and Sean
slipped and fell off the mountain. Sometimes it was one, sometimes
the other that disappeared first over the edge. In a third version they
both fell at the same time. Though I was watching, I was helpless,
unable to act, to move, to do anything to prevent the two of them
from tumbling backwards, over the edge to their deaths twelve hundred feet below.

Once, as this scene played out in my head, I thought back to that
skating episode Thanksgiving weekend when Phil was six, when he
fell through black ice. Now, sixteen years later, I wondered. Had that
been a rehearsal for this final act? At least, I thought, this time we had
all been far from the scene. No one had been there on Mount Rainier
in a position to rescue Phil or not. No question of blame would arise,

91

no issue of responsibility lurking in our marriage bed like a spring bubbling under thin ice.

Thursday came, the day of the memorial service. Out-of-town family members and friends had arrived and begun to gather with us. We sat outside on the deck, chatting with Angus's three sisters. I heard a voice calling my name, looked up and saw in the door a tall figure in a fuchsia shirt and white collar. The voice belonged to my old friend, the former bishop of Minnesota, the one who had mentored me into the Episcopal Church a few years earlier. He and his wife were now living near Chicago, but today he had left their summer place in northern Michigan at dawn to be in Minneapolis for Phil's service.

We took a walk together, winding through the neighborhood on the same route Angus and I had followed the last couple of mornings, one that over the years had become like a walking meditation for me, a path worn deep by the ebb and flow of my spirit. Whereas the route had once been the birthplace of insight, encouraging me day by day on the stages of my spiritual quest, now it received and absorbed nothing but the flow of pain, anxiety, and grief. I poured out to my wise and trusted friend questions that I knew had no answers, but somehow in naming them, there was the promise of direction. "Why had this happened? Why now? Why me? Was this my reward for becoming a Christian? Had the whole conversion process been a preparation for this moment?"

He listened, as usual, with full attention. He urged me not to ask why, only to live the pain, to pray through the grief, to meditate on death—not only Phil's, but my own as well. He urged me to trust that God was "the rock," that in that underlying Unity, that unwavering Presence, I would eventually find solace and a way back into the light.

We were dressing for the service. Nicole came into my room, holding a dress in each hand. One was black, the other splashed with the colors of a summer garden. "Which one should I wear?" she asked. She had good taste, and she always looked nice, but I guessed that clothes were not an important part of Nicole's life, that she did not spend excessive amounts of time thinking about what she wore. I admired her fiercely for it, I who wasted far too much mental energy on the package I wrapped around my body. I remembered Phil, his arm around her, the look of pride he flashed me as we left for a restaurant back in June when they were here. Now I looked at her tenderly. I could feel outrage pushing at me from around the edges. How could it have come to this? How could she be dressing for his *funeral?*

"I think," I said carefully, "that Phil would have loved the flowered one."

We filed into the sanctuary filled with people, into the front pews reserved for family. I kept my eyes before me, looking at the ground. I was shaking, scared, trying to maintain a measure of dignity and control. I sat in the front row, gripping the hand of Angus on one side, of my sister's husband on the other. A cello was offering up intense, rich, melancholy protests that rose to fill the vaulted spaces of the cathedral.

A program was printed for that afternoon, one that Todd's wife Jane had taken charge of, one that I had never seen until that moment. Under Phil's smiling picture was a quote from his final thesis: "If we listen hard enough, you can actually hear creation being silenced and underneath the disappearance of natural sounds resonates an impending groan, a dying heart of a world that has been crucified. If this crucifixion is allowed to continue, God's covenant will never be fulfilled. . . . Humanity must welcome the coming of the 'ecological age' and strive to make the changes while we still have the chance." The program included the text of St. Francis's "Canticle to the Sun," a prayer Phil had quoted in his paper. On the cover, next to his picture, she had placed the drawing of a mountain lupine.

I am the resurrection and the life saith the Lord. . . . From the back of the sanctuary, the bishop's voice rang out, familiar, strong. As he intoned the words of the liturgy in the slow procession, I heard them not as comfort, but as curious hope. I could not accept them now. For me, the question of resurrection was irrelevant. There was only death, blackness, finality, this cross that I was trying to bear. But the words hung there, offered up like a promise, one that I knew I was choosing to ignore. *The Sun of Righteousness is gloriously risen, giving light to those who sat in darkness and in the shadow of death. . . .*

Stew and Dryw, composed and brave but visibly fragile, rose in turn to the microphone to read the selections from Scripture. We had all decided—in the wake of this shock—that none of us should have to speak. We didn't want to add the burden of making a speech to the pain Phil's friends and family had had to endure in the last few days. I appreciated then the value of the *Book of Common Prayer:* that when we are silenced, the wisdom of the ages is collected there to speak for us.

Jean Vail climbed into the pulpit, right above the pew where I was sitting. She looked down into my eyes. I took a deep breath and held it—not daring to exhale into what would be this public attempt to summarize the life and death of my only son. I trusted her, but how could anyone be up to this task? "He was a person to whom people gravitated because of his steadfastness, his fun-loving, upbeat personality, his genuinely accepting, nonjudgmental friendliness. . . ." As I followed her lips, listened to her voice, I realized that all that she had written was perfect. I would have cringed at the slightest note played out of tune, rebelled at the least nuance that didn't ring true. She had read Phil's thesis carefully and used his own words to convey his love of nature, his concern for the environment. As she neared the end of her homily some eight minutes later, I had endorsed every single word she had spoken. At the end, she took us all up onto that icy, slippery mountain where I had spent so many private hours in the days before. "In dying with such heroic generosity of spirit, Philip truly reached for and grasped the hand of God, the life-giving summit."

Just as the congregation began singing "Morning Has Broken," the sun—out from behind a cloud—pierced the honey-stained panes of leaded glass above our heads, filling the cathedral with golden light. Later, several people would write to us of that amazing moment, one that seemed to insist that the words of the liturgy would be fulfilled.

I am standing in the Fireplace Room of the church in a crowd of hundreds of people: friends of Phil's, their parents, friends of ours, friends of Todd and his family. There are Phil's teachers, Angus's business associates, my friends from high school, and two uniformed rangers from Mount Rainier National Park. Nell and Howard have driven back down from the House of Prayer. I feel as if I am being physically held up, passed from one embrace to the other. I lean first on one person, then the next, feeling their arms around me, absorbing their words of sympathy, shock, and pain. I am exhausted, damp in the ninety-degree heat, faint from lack of food.

Suddenly, I am surprised to notice a bubble of pride rise from the empty shell of my heart. How odd. Pride. It is a secret sense of triumph that here I am, actually standing, actually alive and conversing with people when I am living the unthinkable. The worst that can happen has happened, and I can still stand, still talk. There is a hint of power in that, a kernel of hope. It can't ever, ever get worse. I know that. Here I am . . . still me.

At last the crowd had thinned enough for us to leave the church, but at home we found more people waiting. Friends had taken over, organized a buffet supper, invited our closest friends and family to come, to keep the occasion going, to see us all through to the end of the day. One former colleague from work and a tennis partner had flown in from her new home in New York. Just nine months earlier, her husband had died suddenly on the tennis court, playing singles with her. He was fifty-five, lean, and healthy, and his heart had given out with no warning at all. As we were talking, I refused yet another kind person begging me to swallow food. I glanced at my friend. She nodded as if to say, "It's OK not to eat, not now." She understood shock, this pain. I had felt such empathy for her in these months since her husband's death, but now I saw that I had had no inkling of what she had endured.

Another friend was the mother of an only son, about Phil's age. Like me, she was in a second marriage. Her life was full of stepchildren, even stepgrandchildren. But in her eyes, in her quiet presence, I could see a deep resonance rooted in her own vulnerability. She attempted no words of consolation, offered no promises that time would heal. She simply grieved with me, lived this possibility from her own passionate mother love, her own fears.

As the last of the visitors let the screen door slam behind them, I fell onto the couch, drained of the last drop of energy. Our dog Tia came to me, laid her chin in my lap, and searched my face with huge brown eyes. Did she know? Phil was her closest friend, the only one of the kids who had lived with her full-time for weeks on end. He threw the tennis ball the farthest, wrestled with her on the floor, and had trained her by the hour, molding her into an ace Frisbee dog. But how could she know? He hadn't been home for weeks. He was often gone for months. She whined gently, let out a long sigh. She didn't know Phil was dead, but she had sensed the change in the wind.

Friday, the day after the memorial service, was the kind of summer day that makes living in Minnesota worth it, compensating for all the months of snow and cold. The sun shone and sparkled off the lake. The trees swayed in a gentle breeze. For me, now, there could be no joy in it, but the residents of Camp Phil were irrepressible. A motor whined in the distance, then two, then three. The boats pulled up at our dock and a knot of Phil's buddies appeared on the front lawn.

"We've been to the Arcola bridge," they shouted up at me. "We all did a jump for Phil. Even Cha. It was a real rush."

I looked at Jeff, new to Minnesota, to this lake scene, clearly not a young man inclined to jumping off high bridges. "Even me," he echoed proudly.

The Arcola bridge is an old railroad bridge, a high span over the water of Lake Minnetonka, connecting two spits of land. Its iron sides resting on wooden trestles are layered with aged graffiti, memorializing scores of high school sweethearts dating back several decades. The boat traffic under the bridge is heavy at certain times during the week, but on a weekday morning like this one, plenty of opportunity would be available for the boys to gather their courage, hold their noses, and plunge about forty feet into the channel below.

I looked at the boys, some Minnesota natives, high school friends who had performed this ritual for years, others visitors from out of state like Jeff. The image of those young bodies hurtling off that bridge into the water brought up an old familiar panic, took me back to the years of cliff and bungee jumping. *At least Phil wasn't with them*, I thought, until I remembered I had no more reason to fear for him now.

As that harrowing mental tape of Mount Rainier continued to play over and over in my head, the vision was slowly turning into a version that I could handle. After one of them slipped, Phil or Sean, Sean or Phil, they fell. Roped together, they fell—not fifty feet like a cliff or seventy-five feet like a hot-air balloon, but *twelve hundred feet*. They fell, their voices rising in a banshee yell, echoing into the wind that whistled over the glacier. It was free fall, floating flight, the ultimate rush, ending in the soft snow below, their spirits long since released into the August night.

The boys would be hungry now, after their morning adventure. I knew they would be looking for lunch. Just then the phone rang: Jane Barry, calling to tell me that Camp Phil had run out of food. Did we have any more? We didn't have enough to feed this crowd. The reception after the service the night before had pretty well wiped us out. I put down the receiver, exhausted by the thought of having to do something about it, in a near panic at the thought of thirty or so young people looking for lunch.

We heard the beep of a truck backing down our driveway. I ran to the window and saw a phalanx of people delivering boxes to our front door. The secretaries in Angus's office had joined forces to send us food. There were warm buns and sliced loaves of bread, deli trays of meats and cheese, tomatoes and lettuce, mustard, mayonnaise, fruit, and a box of freshly baked cookies. I took a deep breath of gratitude and called down to the dock. "Come on in, all of you. Lunch is ready!"

After lunch, our family, Nicole and Jeff, Stew and Dryw, piled into cars to drive to a small, private burial service. As Angus drove, Nicole handed me a cassette tape from the back seat, a mix of songs Phil had made for her, and she asked me to play it. One particular song, she said, she wanted us to hear. The song, by Marc Cohn, was called "True Companion."

"Yes, I'll climb a mountain," he sang, "I'm gonna swim the sea. There ain't no act of God, girl, could keep you safe from me." The haunting, soulful refrain kept repeating that she was his long-sought "true companion." After he told of having his heart set on their wedding day, of his vision of her in white, how he dreamed of lifting her veil with trembling hands, he sang:

Then when I leave this Earth
I'll be with the angels standin'
I'll be out there waiting
for my true companion.

Soon we were all drawn by the music down into a place deep inside that had been walled off by the sun of the morning, the boats, the shouts, the lunch, and the stories. Phil was with us now—his absence was with us—in a visceral, no longer abstract way.

The extended family was waiting when we drove through the cemetery gates: nieces and nephews, their spouses, grandparents, Todd's family as well. The ashes had arrived from Seattle, and one of the cemetery staff handed Angus and me, then Todd, each a small plastic bag of ashes that we had requested be kept separate, destined for other places. I felt a metal object being placed in my hand. It was a ring, Phil's ring, of that there was no doubt. It had been a birthday gift to him from Nicole, a mixed metal band of intricate design. I turned the ring slowly in my hand, this clear evidence that there could be no mistaking the body they had found. I imagined the warm, dear flesh that had penetrated its shape only six days before. I saw a doctor, the medical examiner, wondering at its significance, removing it carefully from a lifeless finger. I squeezed it tightly one last time, then touched Nicole's shoulder and slipped the ring gently into her hand.

We all drove to the gravesite and gathered quietly under the trees on that hot, sticky, calm day. On an impulse, I had brought a vase of twenty-two peach-colored roses—one for each of Phil's years—that had been sent by a group of girls, friends from Bates who had not been able to come to Minneapolis. I took the roses from the vase and passed them out, one to each person as long as they held out. Phil's grave, a site we had chosen two days before, was on a grassy knoll, under spreading branches of aged oak trees.

The grave was at the Wurtele family site, where Angus's parents were buried, where he and I, his children, his sisters, and their families would also be laid some day. A fresh hole had been dug in the ground, surrounded by pieces of green Astroturf to hide the newly turned earth, to give a formal, dressy feel to the occasion. Jean was robed in white, an embroidered stole around her neck, a prayer book in her hand. *For so did you ordain when you created me, saying, you are dust and to dust you shall return.*

*Angus and I, Todd and Jane are kneeling together at the edge of the grave.
We are each holding a corner of a simple bronze box. The box is heavy. I suddenly understand that in this box is my son. The heaviness I feel is his skin,
his bones, his muscle, his vital organs. A huge howling pain rises up in me. I
can't, won't let go of the box. The others get up. I stay there on my knees,
leaning down into the hole. I feel my own weight being drawn down, down.
I want to let my hold on life go slack. I want to be a rose, tossed on to his
grave, to drift petal by petal, down to mingle with this earth that will be his
bed until the end of time. The words of the prayer book reverberated: "All of
us go down to the dust; yet even at the grave, we make our song."*

*At last I stand up. A cool breeze stirs. It tosses the branches of the trees
overhead, swells our skirts and the priest's robe, ruffles our hair. He is here,
I think, in the wind, flesh no more.*

On the way home, we stopped at the farmer stand, loading dozens of
ears of Minnesota sweet corn into the car. We boiled them in huge
kettles of water and offered steaming platters of them to the groups of
friends who lingered still, the college kids, the Barrys, freed at last
from their labors next door. As the sun set over the lake, we chatted
and regaled each other with Phil stories.

I was glad that Phil's high school girlfriend Elizabeth stayed on
with us a while longer. She was Nicole's predecessor, and, as I watched
the two of them talking together, discovering how much they had in
common, I wondered at Phil's history with women. How had he come
to love so deeply, so young? At times, I had worried that he was too
serious about his women. I thought he might do better to play the
field. Now, in the wake of his death, I felt only gratitude that he had
known love, both physically and emotionally.

Elizabeth and Nicole liked each other; they had discovered a
number of common bonds. They were the same age, both a year
older than Phil. They both drove 1986 Jettas, loved to camp, to hike.

Elizabeth had just finished a summer job as a youth guide, leading a group of students up Mount Rainier just weeks before. She had had no idea that Phil was a ranger there that summer.

As we leaned over the kitchen counter talking together that night, Elizabeth looked at me. "Let's go fly fishing some day, the three of us," she suggested. Then I knew these two women could be part of a new life I would try to build out of the ashes.

CHAPTER 12

New Family

Now he's gone, and the family has to restructure
itself. . . . We have to live around the gap. Take one
out and everything changes.

Nicholas Wolterstorff

Now we were alone, our new family of five. Until then, we had always
been six when we were all together. We were six, but Phil and I had
been a kind of unit, a subdivision defined by flesh and blood. I had
drawn strength from that liaison. His presence had bestowed a kind of
legitimacy on my role as "mother." My stepchildren, of course, had a
mother of their own, but when we were together as a group, I func-
tioned in that role.

Phil had brought me into the sisterhood of mothers. He had
awakened me to the powerful feelings, the physical, almost animal
possessiveness of parenting.

Now I considered the family landscape, primarily Angus and his
three children. The lay of the land had changed. I felt unmistakably,
undeniably alone. I no longer had my ally, my buddy, the only one I
knew loved me unconditionally. I no longer had a child of my own.
How could I possibly go on? Who would care for me? Who would

look after me and love me when I was old, sick, or no longer useful? Who would love me *now*? I felt a swirling vortex of pain where Phil used to be. That place of hope, of dreams that anchored me to the future, that promised me grandchildren and great-grandchildren was now a dead end, a void. I was untethered, floating, a flesh-and-blood universe of one.

I considered my stepchildren. When they were eight, eleven, and twelve, their world had fallen apart. Their mother was feeling constrained by her marriage. She needed her freedom, to find a new life in which she could regain the youth and independence of which she felt she had been deprived. At first, she and Angus had alternated three-month periods, living in their house with the children. Finally, when divorce was inevitable, Angus had to find a place of his own. He and I began to see each other in those months he lived alone. A year later, we decided to marry and bought a new house together, just down the hill from where his ex-wife and children were living. A year after our wedding, she decided she needed still more independence and adventure. She moved out of state, to Aspen, Colorado, and Heidi, Andrew, and Chris moved in with us full-time. Phil was five.

Before they all moved in, in the first year of our marriage, Angus and I had considered the possibility of having a child of our own. I had never imagined that I would go through life with only one child. I considered Phil's need for a "real" sibling, my own need for a backup in case something should ever happen to him. Angus was eleven years my senior. He was just about to turn forty-two when we married, but his own father had been fifty when Angus, the youngest of five, was born. I was still only thirty-two. He was entirely willing to have another child, and he left the decision up to me.

In the midst of our deliberations, my best friend Nancy gave birth to her second child. The day of the birth was a joyous celebration, the boy for whom she had been hoping. Now, with her daughter Sasha, the family was complete, perfect. The morning of the second day she called me from the hospital again. Her voice was slow, heavy. "They think he has Down's syndrome," she said. "There are a few more tests, but I'm afraid it looks likely."

I remember traveling to Mexico City with Angus for a meeting later that week. I was awakened at dawn in a strange hotel room, jarred into consciousness by my own huge, gulping sobs. I had had a dream in which I had a baby who died. It wasn't Phil, I knew that. But as I gave vent to the pain and grief I was feeling that morning, I clearly knew what the dream meant. The time had come to let go of the vision of more children, to acknowledge that I would have no more babies. I had seen my best friend's life be forever altered by this new birth. I had not only one son, but three healthy stepchildren. I needed to accept that this was it. I felt such pain, such grief at the prospect of no other children, but I knew that in our situation the right decision was made.

Now, eighteen years later, I wondered. What if I *had* had another child? How would I be feeling now? Angus and I had reflected on our decision many times over the years. We had always felt there was a nice balance in the family the way it was: all four of the children had had to suffer through divorce. If we had had one of our own, that youngest child would live with both parents, to be envied if not resented by the other four. He had three, and I had one, but Phil was a lot younger; he would be around to live with us for years longer. We never talked about the other possibility, the one good reason to try again: the thought that Phil could die.

Looking back, I knew it didn't matter. Having a child had made me so vulnerable. I had always known that, always looked at it as the price to be paid for love. But having another would have made me *twice* as exposed, not half as vulnerable. Having another child could not in any measure have lessened the pain I was feeling now. Phil was one soul, one unique human being that I had lost irrevocably. Another child would only have meant that yet another person in the family would have to grieve.

I remembered the first time I had really considered Phil's place in the family constellation. In the spring of his third-grade year, Phil and I were touring a new school. His public Montessori program had been great for the first few years, but it had seemed to encourage creativity to the detriment of spelling and grammar. I had begun to worry that he would never catch up with other students his age. We were visiting a fourth-grade classroom in the independent school that I myself had attended for several years.

"Mom, I can't go to this school." Phil waved me over to a corner of the room where a chart hung on the wall. The names of all the children in the class were listed on the left. Four columns followed the names: "youngest," "oldest," "middle" and "only child." Opposite each child's name a star had been glued in the column that represented his or her place in the family.

"What do you mean you can't go here?" I asked. He pointed to the chart.

"But I'm *all* of those," he said. "I'm the youngest at home and the oldest at Dad's. I'm really in the middle of them all, and I'm your only child." He was right, of course, and I wondered if he would be the only child in the class from a blended family.

In our house, no doubt about it, Phil had been the youngest. Five years younger than Heidi, he was the lowest of the low. One morning, Heidi had come downstairs in the morning, rubbing sleep from her eyes. "Dad, I dreamed last night that you and Mom got back together, but"—she looked at me encouragingly—"Margaret and Phil still lived next door." They didn't really mind having this new little brother around, and one more was available down the chain to treat as siblings naturally do.

Occasionally—like any little brother—Phil was teased and tortured by the older kids. I knew, in a way, that they were waiting for me to defend my flesh and blood at any cost. I also knew that if I were ever to gain my stepchildren's acceptance and affection, I couldn't always be on Phil's side. At times I even told him privately why I had to do that, to stay neutral. I think he understood that he needed to be—in the context of our new family—the youngest of four, not one against three. The four of them grew to love and respect each other, in spite of the turf wars that established a pecking order. I knew, as the years passed, that for Phil to be put in his place, to learn to defend his slot in the world, was healthy. "Which one do you really *feel* like, inside?" I asked, as we looked together years later at that chart on the classroom wall. "Youngest," he answered matter-of-factly, and we turned and left the room.

Now the youngest was gone, excised from the family that we had all known for eighteen years. Chris was going to fly back to Colorado the next morning. We called everyone together. We had discussed what to do with Phil's ashes, the ones we had kept apart after the burial. We all knew that the cemetery was a convention, one that we had chosen to provide a permanent marking place, but it was one that might not have appealed to Phil. Phil would, we thought, probably want some of them scattered on Mount Rainier, the place he had loved so much and where he had spent such a peaceful last summer of his life. But this place was the focus of our family life, the place we would come back to, all of us, as long as we lived. Didn't it seem right to leave some of him here?

The sun was nearing the horizon, and some of the oppressive heat of the day was lifting. We gathered together, the five of us, on the lawn. I had searched the cupboards and found a simple earthen pottery bowl. I emptied most of the bag of ashes into it, reserving a little for a future trip to Mount Rainier and some for Chris, who had asked to take them back to the mountains in Colorado where he and Phil had hiked together. I held the bowl, no longer an abstract weight, but the very skin and bones I had longed to touch and to see. I dipped my fingers into the powdery substance, rubbed them together to feel their grit, the presence of this absent son, letting it lodge under my nails. As the sun glowed orange over the lake, we took turns scattering handfuls into the evening breeze. *Ashes to ashes, dust to dust. . . .* On this sacred ground of home, we offered them up to nourish the blades of grass that would be a carpet under our feet, cushion Tia's afternoon naps, and feed the rabbits who passed our way. There was relief and a sense of completion in this ritual. Rather than stowing him away in an impenetrable box, we had brought him home at last, surrounding ourselves with this essence of a life.

As the light of day faded slowly into dusk, I felt as if I was taking some first tentative breaths. In these last few days, I felt as if I had been frantically resuscitated from my own kind of death. The experience had been intense, touch and go, as if I had been receiving artificial respiration that kept me alive just enough to make it through these frenzied events in the wake of Phil's death. Now I felt as if I could begin to breathe on my own.

The air filled with a delicious smell as Andrew and Chris grilled the vegetables and Angus tended to the chicken. Heidi and I set the table, cut a bouquet of red and white snapdragons and yellow coreopsis from the garden.

That day was our eighteenth wedding anniversary, something Angus and I had both completely forgotten.

CHAPTER 13

Convergence

In order to let us be free, in order to let us be human,
God has to leave us free to choose.

Rabbi Harold Kushner

I spread out a week-old copy of the *New York Times*. I wanted to
spend time with an article that I had barely glanced at the day it was
published. There, under photographs of Sean and Phil, was the headline "Two Young Men Who Loved Mountains Lost Their Lives on
One." Phil's picture was his high school senior portrait, the same one
we had used on the program for the memorial service. His blond hair
cut short, the bangs brushed to one side, he looked right into the camera. Fresh-faced, young, he was the all-American boy next door. In
the four years since the photo had been taken, Phil's hair had curled a
bit around the edges. His jaw had a wider, more mature set. He
looked, at the end, more like a man than the photo suggested.

I stared at the photograph of Sean. His hair, darker than Phil's,
was pulled back in a ponytail. He looked slightly down, away from the
camera with a dreamy-eyed look as if he were far away. His lean face
looked open and sincere, and I knew, studying the picture, that Sean

was kind, gentle, and sensitive. The article said that, like Phil, Sean was idealistic and committed to "caring for the earth." He had become an enthusiastic climber in his freshman year at the University of California at Santa Cruz, from which he had just graduated in June. He loved the mountains, writing about them in a letter to his parents earlier that summer, one that was quoted in the article: "The snow has all melted out around my camp, unleashing both green grass and beautiful purple, red, white and yellow wildflowers. . . ." I could not stop gazing at Sean's picture, could not stop fury pushing up at the thought of this other priceless young life, lost forever.

My sister called when she saw the article in the *New York Times.* "Think of it this way," she said gently. The fact that my only child had died was earthshaking, primal. The loss was so deep, so huge, that— like any mother in the same position—I wanted to put my chin in the air and howl, howl so loudly that everyone in the world could hear; howl it to the oceans, to the mountains, to the stars. I wanted the world to stop and take note. I wanted them all—everyone—to mourn from coast to coast. I wanted the earth to stop turning on its axis. "Just think," she said. "You almost have that." Phil's death had been widely reported both on television and in the newspapers in Washington, in Minneapolis, on Paul Harvey's radio program, and now the *New York Times.* "It can't lessen the grief," my sister said, "but it must be satisfying to know your horrible news is being heard."

Sean's parents, Judy and Bill, had called us on one of the first mornings after the accident from their home on the Hudson River in South Nyack, New York. They had been camping themselves in Jackson Hole, Wyoming, the week before. They had finished their planned time in the wilderness and hiked out, back into one of the public reception areas of the national park. They had noticed a flag at half-mast and wondered who could have died while they had been out of touch. Just then, they saw their daughter coming toward them. She had heard the news about Sean and chartered a small plane from

Colorado to be there when they came out, to tell them the news personally. That flag was flying—as were all of the flags at national parks that day—at half-mast for Sean and Phil.

As we talked, we could hear in their voices the same shock, help-lessness, and pain that we felt, engulfed as we were in this identical nightmare. The ropes that had bound our two sons in death now seemed to reach across the country to pull us together in our grief.

A videotape had arrived in the mail, sent by Todd's brother Pock. The note enclosed with the tape explained that it was a recording of two interviews he had filmed of his nephew Phil, one when he was twelve years old, the other a couple of days after his high school graduation. I took the tape greedily in my hand. Here was a precious gift: at least an hour of Phil on a tape that I had never known existed. I couldn't look at it right away, but eventually I could resist no longer.

At eighteen, Phil had grown out of his baby face, into a square-jawed, handsome young man with an easy smile. He was relaxed, funny. He told stories about the all-night graduation party he had just survived, about his efforts to land a summer job, about the twenty-two-hundred-mile bike trip he and Dryw had taken to California fourth quarter as their senior project. Finally his uncle asked him, "Do you see yourself settling down in Minnesota some day?" "Well," he replied, "Minnesota is great, but it would be perfect if it had mountains. I love mountains so much. I love looking at them; I love exploring them. I think I'll have to live near the mountains. There are mountains in Maine, but if Bates were in Tacoma, Washington, then I'd really be happy." He looked dreamily off camera. "It's right near Mount Rainier. . . . I'd love to climb it some day." Incredibly, the tape ran out and the interview ended on that sentence.

I was reading mail one day when the phone rang. As usual, I hesitated before answering. I needed energy to respond, to reassure whoever was calling that yes, it was a good time to call, to help them through the discomfort I knew they felt, searching for words of comfort and sympathy.

"Hello?"

The words coming through the phone were jumbled, low, barely audible. I listened hard, asked the man please to repeat his name.

"This is John Craven, calling from California." *John Craven . . . John Craven.* I recognized the name, but I couldn't put a face to it. Then, in a flash, I knew. John Craven was the man who had broken his ankle on Mount Rainier, the man whose life Phil and Sean had been trying to save. My breath caught. I had wondered for days whether I would ever hear from him. I had tried to imagine what it would be like to be John Craven, to know that two young men had died trying to reach him on that cold, icy night. I felt anger rise from the pit of my stomach, fury that this man on the other end of the phone was alive, that his ankle would heal, that I would never hear my son's voice again.

He told me how sorry he was that Phil had died, how much he appreciated what he and Sean had done for him. As he spoke, his words carefully composed, his voice full of fear and pain, my heart opened to him. I knew how hard this call was, how much courage it must have taken. I knew too that he needed desperately to do this, to acknowledge his fortune and his debt, to reach out to us. I had known all along how important this connection was, both for John Craven and for me.

I thought hard about the possibilities. Phil could have been up there on the mountain, freezing through a long, dark night. Phil, in shock and pain, could have been waiting for a rescue crew. Phil could have learned at dawn that because of him two people had died.

"I'm glad you called," I said. "It must have been hard. Even if you hadn't called, I was planning to write you, to tell you that we don't hold anything against you personally." I hung up the phone, shaking, wondering if, for the rest of his days, John Craven would measure his life against the two that were lost for him.

Todd and his daughter Katie flew out to Seattle to attend a public memorial service for Sean and Phil. We were grateful to them for going, for being a family presence there. Sean's uncle Tony and his daughter Caroline were there too. A small memorial service was held on the mountain a couple of days before, just for Park Service employees. This second, public service took place on the campus of the University of Washington in Seattle. Todd called to tell us about it. A single bagpipe played "Amazing Grace," and a huge American flag flew above the square, called Rainier Vista. The mountain was obscured by a bank of clouds. Near the lectern, four uniformed rangers stood silently, at attention, holding ice axes, helmets, and crampons, symbols of their fallen colleagues. Todd said there were sad, heartfelt eulogies. He remembered one man in particular, a man of thirty-three, who came up to him after the service. He said he had spent a summer on the mountain, a ranger himself, when he was Phil's age. He had then gone to medical school and become a doctor, but in his mind, his time on Mount Rainier had unquestionably been the highlight of his life.

In the second week, Angus and I took a couple of days and drove up to the House of Prayer. David Keller had called earlier in the week to invite us to come. I had not spoken with him since we drove off from his house on that horrible Monday afternoon. Measured, serene, David's voice had always had wonderful associations for me, a source of wisdom and guidance. Now my reaction was different. Hearing his voice again on the telephone, I had felt a knot beginning to form in my stomach. How could I go back there and be with him again, look into those same eyes, the same face that had delivered the message that ruined my life? But as we talked, I could see that he was right. We did need to do that, to go right back up there, to exorcise the demons that were beginning to cluster around a place that had been such a positive part of my life.

I was a board member of the House of Prayer, and it was understood that I would be taking over as head of the board at the annual meeting in the spring. I had committed to lead a major fund drive on the horizon as well. All of that, however, paled next to the fact that the House of Prayer was central to my spiritual life. It was a peaceful, valuable place of retreat, where I had spent long weekends in silent meditation, where I had sat at the foot of wise, thoughtful people who were mentors and guides for me along the path. That this place should become a pit of negative energy and despair was simply not acceptable. So we headed up there, to the House of Prayer, situated on land owned by St. John's abbey, a Benedictine monastery in Collegeville, about an hour and a half northeast of home.

The lake behind the abbey was placid, a mirror image of the August afternoon sky, wreathed with lush forest and marshland. Angus and I made our way slowly along a trail that traces the rim of the lake, up and down hills, over rickety wooden bridges, under the cool shade of ancient trees. Our destination was Stella Maris, an old stone chapel that beckons from a promontory on the far shore, opposite the abbey church. Every quarter hour, as we walked hand in hand, the abbey bells tolled, marking the passage of time. The ringing had a gentle, insistent rhythm. Just as we felt ourselves beginning to sink inexorably back into the anxiety and obsessions this grief had engulfed us in, the bells broke through, reminding us of another realm, a mysterious reality that permeates the everyday world in which we were drowning.

We paused to watch turtles sunning themselves on logs, listened to the whine of cicadas slicing like buzz saws into the heat and silence that hung over the lake. At last, hot and tired, we reached the chapel.

Though small, it was commanding, a proud relic of the abbey's decades-long presence. The interior was small, housing only a stone altar, with arched openings in the fieldstone walls we could lean on to look out at the lake. In front of the chapel, steep steps led directly down to the water. We followed them, and there, beneath our own reflections, we could see through the shallow water to a bottom that was sandy and smooth. It was irresistible. We quickly stripped down and slipped our bodies into the crystal-clear, cool water. The feeling was delicious—a first, shocking sensation of pleasure that, just for an instant, pierced through the dull numbness that had encased my body for a week.

On the way back, we stopped, frozen in our steps. On the path ahead of us was a fawn that looked at us, unafraid, with huge brown eyes, its big ears turned our way as if to test the nature of our presence. We must have been reassuring, for it made no move to run away, but settled in and began to nibble the underbrush lining the trail. I thought of Phil, of his last days at Glacier Basin, of the deer who gathered near his campsite. Soon a second fawn emerged from the brush, and they both stayed there together, peaceful and unafraid. Finally, we began to move slowly by them. They never ran or took flight. I felt raw, open, as if Phil's attraction to wild things had surfaced from inside of me, as if I was seeing with his eyes, exuding his aura of trust.

That night Angus, David, and I drove to a restaurant in a town several miles from the abbey and the House of Prayer. At a table by a window overlooking the gently flowing Sauk River, we spent three hours together. I looked long and hard at David's face. I took in the lean lines, the light-colored, slightly graying straight hair, the kind blue eyes, the thin lips, the gentle smile. I considered the message, then the messenger; I tried to separate the two. Breaking the news of Phil's death, David said, was the hardest thing he had ever had to do in his forty years of ministry. I forgave him. More than that, I found gratitude buried underneath the fear of this reunion. How lucky I was that I had been here where I had been, in such safe hands, to receive the news. Being there at that time was a gift. Now I could understand that and be thankful.

That night I told David about the fear I had lived with for years, how I had always, at some level, had a sense that something would happen to Phil, more than the usual worry that mothers have. My sense was a kind of quiet, secret *certainty* of a different order. I told him how I had tried to force the thoughts away, to vaporize them, but how it had led ultimately to the completeness I now felt about my relationship with my son. I told David too about Jean Vail, about my tears in Chicago. I reminded him of my strange experience in meditation that fateful Monday morning at the House of Prayer, when Phil was already dead but we didn't know it. How had I *known* before I knew?

David's response was slow, measured, thoughtful. I think we are trapped, he mused, in time and space, but they are not what they seem. There is a greater unity to all things than we are privileged to perceive. Now and then—particularly if we engage in regular spiritual practice that opens us, makes us more receptive—we are permitted a glimpse that transcends linear time and space. Perhaps these premonitions had been examples of these lifts into a realm beyond our normal consciousness, a realm in which we are touched by the truth that passes all understanding. Past, present, and future are not what they appear to be. Nor is distance the separation it seems.

I pressed on. What does it mean to talk of "God's will"? So many people were writing to us of some sort of cosmic plan, one that would eventually come clear, that would finally reveal why Phil had been "chosen" to die. In a recent sermon Jean Vail had decried the tendency people have to feel blessed or chosen when they receive an A on a test or when a parking place mysteriously appears: "elevating coincidences to miracles." The corollary of that way of thinking is that God selected Phil to fall off the mountain or Nancy to get cancer.

The thought that this outcome had somehow been planned tortured me. No, like Jean, David did not believe that God is a micromanager. God is the overreaching, undergirding texture of all things, the One, not the many; the Whole, not the pieces; the Harmony, not the individual notes.

I thought, as I reflected on his words, that the important thing is to have reverence for the mystery. I knew only that the world works in strange ways: not chaotic, not random, not logical either. There is a dance. There is a convergence—of events, of meaning. There is powerful coincidence, powerful irony. Perhaps that is enough.

We woke at dawn and drove with David back to the lake. In a gentle rain, we made our way down a thickly wooded path to the shore where he stowed his canoe, a beautifully crafted one in dark green with wooden gunnels and woven cane seats. Angus and David paddled out into the mist with me sitting in the middle, along for the ride. As we glided along in the half-light, a loon appeared in our path. It let us approach, then flapped its wings in a show of welcome. Further on, we came to a baby loon, now nearly full-size but still gray and unfinished in its ruffled feather costume. A deer in the woods raised its head to watch us pass; a great blue heron stood motionless along the shore. We must have threatened to scare the fish that the heron was watching. It took off, huge blue wings beating a slow rise over our heads. Just as we pulled up on shore, thunder rolled. Rain pattered in earnest on the water behind us and on the thick canopy of leaves that kept us dry as we ran for the car.

Back home, exactly two weeks had passed since Phil's death. I had slept, now, two whole nights without pills—a dull, black, dreamless sleep. I woke exhausted, as if I had not even put my head down. Heidi, Nicole, and Phil's high school girlfriend Elizabeth had all told me about dreams of Phil. Nicole had been on a ferryboat on a river when he called on the phone. She could see his face and he was smiling. She said, "Where *are* you?" He didn't answer, but she could hear him talking to Sean on his end of the line.

Elizabeth dreamed that she sat with Phil on a rock face in Washington. She told him she had been on Mount Rainier and that he had died. He gave her a big smile and asked her if she had reached the summit. She said yes, and he gave her a hug.

Heidi dreamed that the whole family was sitting around the table in the dining room, mourning. Phil appeared and made his way around the table, greeting each person, hugging first one, then the other, repeating to each, "I'm sorry, I'm so, so sorry."

Where was Phil? Why did I not dream of him? Was he keeping his distance, unable to approach his mother, repelled by her tears, the pain, the agony?

My friend Marcia called from New York, the one whose husband had died suddenly on the tennis court. She had come through Minneapolis again, en route home from their cabin in northern Minnesota. She and her grown children had taken her husband's ashes to Lakewood Cemetery to bury them, eleven months to the day after his death. When they had finished their family ceremony, she had asked to be shown to Phil's grave. Their car followed the winding road through the bright green acres studded with large stone monuments, shaded by huge old trees. At last they came to the landmark where they had been told to park; they stepped out and walked toward the Wurtele plot. There, standing silently, right on Phil's grave, was a magnificent buck deer.

CHAPTER 14

Earthly Things

I think every parent must have a sense of failure, even of sin, in remaining alive after the death of a child.

Frances Gunther

Now it was just the two of us. Angus and I had been living together alone for months, for years really, since Phil had gone off to college, but now—two weeks after his death—it felt, in a way, like we were alone for the first time. Our marriage found itself in a new landscape, one we didn't recognize. The dynamics had changed; so had the cast of characters. We knew we needed time away to become used to it all, to try to feel our way into a new kind of relationship, one grounded in loss and pain. We needed to see whether the relationship had a future that could grow beyond this loneliness and desolation.

We accepted an invitation from good friends to use their summer retreat on Lake Superior for a few days. We drove four hours north and settled into the simple log cabin with its stone fireplace, big screen porch, and wide deck with a view of the water. The time was one of isolation, reading, preparing simple meals, walking in the woods.

On our walks, I found that my way of seeing had clearly changed. As we negotiated the wet, muddy path, the footholds encircled by tree roots seemed not to jump up at me in fascinating detail as they usually did, but just to fade, to flatten into one long, grainy, monotonous cinematic backdrop. The plentiful mushrooms that dotted the woods, black, bordered, and speckled, blended into an undistinguished blur. A few, tinged with a luminous scarlet, sent up flares to try to awaken my dulled and unresponsive spirit, but to no avail.

Angus braved an afternoon swim in the frigid waters of Lake Superior. I watched, glazed and uninterested, from the deck. Afterwards, his body cold and tight, he came up behind me, laid his freezing hands on my cheeks and invited me to come to bed with him.

The thought of sex repulsed me. How could I ever again engage in that act that was all about having children when my only one was dead? Sex at that moment seemed a cruel mockery. How could I even think about physical pleasure when the whole world was filled with pain? Still, I knew that this marriage was my lifeline, that my husband's love was the single most important thing left to me. I had been reading, distractedly, a book Nicole had recommended, Jeanette Winterson's *Written on the Body*. Perhaps the racy prose I had just ingested might stir some long-forgotten desire. I stood up and followed him.

The lovemaking was a disaster. His touch felt like sandpaper on raw nerve. I couldn't relax. I felt violated. Anger and resentment flared that he could even think of pleasuring himself. He gave up, leaving me lying on the bed, dissolved in tears. They were tears of loneliness, of emptiness, acknowledging that sex, for me and for my female body, had come to naught, that its only product was wiped out, reduced to ashes.

I tried to meditate at dawn, as I had for so many weeks and months before, but now I was afraid of the inner darkness, afraid to quiet my mind and journey downward, to close my eyes and ears and open myself to inner space. I was afraid of the pain I might find there, afraid of discovering a well as deep as the core of the earth. Instead, we lay awake talking each morning, pressed together in the narrow twin bed in the cabin's spare room.

Each day I spent a couple of hours answering mail. We had brought with us a large wicker basket stuffed to the brim with envelopes of varying colors and sizes. The basket held typed letters, formal monogrammed notes, carefully selected sympathy cards, exquisitely penned messages on fringed handmade paper; letters from dear, close friends, others from mere acquaintances; notes from people we had not seen for years, for decades, some from names we could not even remember; letters from complete strangers, forwarded to us by the Park Service, residents of Washington moved by the story of the two young men they had read about in the newspapers.

As I contemplated the basket, I was reminded of a conversation with a good friend earlier in the summer. She told me she had written a note to a prominent theater artist in the community on the death of his mother. She didn't know him well, but she had been moved to write. She had struggled mightily with every sentence, almost given up. But in the end, she had finished the note and mailed it. "Do you know," she had confided to me, "he never even acknowledged it? Not one word."

I could feel the love, the careful effort represented by the jumble of paper spilling out of that basket. It was clear to me that I needed to respond to every one, no matter how long it took. I began with notes to the people who had come with food and flowers, who had taken time to visit with us in those first few days. As I wrote, working off the lists that my mother and Gail had kept for us, I began to sense the value in the writing. "I *will* heal," I penned, in one note after another, "I *will* heal, because Phil would have it no other way." I could see that this repetitive action, this writing a single phrase over and over, would work like a mantra, a process of positive affirmation that could—even though I didn't really believe it now—make itself true over time.

It was the last morning of our stay. We took a four-and-a-half-mile hike along the Split Rock Trail, up one side of the river, down the other. This day the world was a little less flat. I noticed the bird calls, felt the wind against my skin, let the rushing of the water lull my brain into peaceful thoughts. I considered this man walking beside me. Though he had a decade's head start, he seemed no older than I was. Lean, muscular at sixty, he looked two-thirds his age. His straight, blondish hair was thin on top, but no gray had yet appeared, no paunch was visible at the belt line.

Eighteen years we had lived together. We had struggled with long hours of work, with the challenges of a blended family of four children. Our energy levels were matched; our interests had grown together. Since Phil's death, Angus had seemed to have an infinite capacity to listen to me, to let me give vent to my feelings without running away from the ugliness of the grief, without trying to talk me out of the pain. I could see that he was truly grieving himself, something I might not have counted on, and that was a gift as well.

The clouds burned off and were gone by the time we drove home from our hike. We sat for a last lunch in the sun on the deck, overlooking the vast expanse of Lake Superior. A chickadee serenaded us from a tall pine nearby. Then we settled in to read.

After an hour or so, Angus came up to me, out of his shady spot over to my chair in the sun. His hands were cool, stroking my shoulders, massaging my neck. I knew what his gentle overture meant. I felt resistance beginning to rise, but I also knew he was right, that our marriage depended upon renewing our bond of flesh. I had heard that divorces were common after the death of a child, and I couldn't bear even the thought that we might drift apart. If we didn't break through now, we risked alienation forever.

I followed him into the bedroom, fell reluctantly onto the narrow mattress. I felt torn, full of shame, as if this pleasure seeking were a violation of Phil's memory. Even as hot tears welled up and rolled down my face, I forced myself to relax into the familiar patterns, let the earth undulate with me, the secret needs of my pent-up body ride the rhythm of the waves. They broke at last, the pleasure, like relief, pulsing through me. Not until afterwards, lying quietly, did I begin to cry out loud.

It is still August, a Tuesday morning. I pass a mirror, stop, stare hard at the face in the glass. How can that be me? I wonder. She looks like I used to look, but what has happened to the person inside? I used to be so happy, so cheerful, fulfilled. Now those eyes are haunted. The mouth is tense, turned down. All that I thought about, dreamed about, cared about, has been displaced, rendered irrelevant.

Nothing lay in front of us that September but the thing I dreaded most in the world: normal life. We had to go on. We had no alternative but to begin. The life I had led up until the fateful weekend with the house guests was still there waiting for me. I appeared the same on the outside, but I was entirely new.

Going to the grocery store required monumental effort. I wore sunglasses, skulked around the ends of aisles, tried to glimpse around a corner to see whom I should try to avoid. Each person I met required a lifetime of energy, and I had none to give. Did they know? If they did, would they bring it up? If they didn't bring it up, was it because they knew and chickened out, or because they didn't know? If they didn't know, should I tell them, ruin their day? If they did bring it up, then it was agony—on my part and theirs—deciding what to say. Should I acknowledge the pain or should I ease theirs, strike an optimistic note and reassure them that I would heal? I desperately needed people to know, to share my pain, but I couldn't bear the effort it took to receive the support. I returned home exhausted from every foray out of the house.

All I wanted to do was to stay home where I was safe, where I could cry and grieve as the urge struck, or choose not to without being judged.

At home was the mountain of mail to be answered. The baskets, now two of them, were stuffed with hundreds of notes, but I couldn't seem to make myself sit down to write. People had sent books, but reading was impossible. I had no desire to cook, no interest in food. All I could do was walk, cry, and remember. I wrote in my journal and worked on a needlepoint I had started. That task allowed me to feel productive when I had neither the energy nor the concentration for anything else. I could thread the needle with colored yarn, weave it in and out of the tiny waxed squares in the canvas, follow the patterns up and down, and let my mind run, searching for Phil, trying to picture his face, to hold on to the shreds of memory that appeared briefly, then faded away.

I was desperately afraid that I would forget Phil. I would sit on the floor, spread out in a big collage on the living room carpet the photographs that people had sent to us. Then, if I squinted my eyes just right, moved them quickly over the pile, I imagined I could see him there, watch him move, see him smiling, winking, staring, laughing. But then I would catch myself, see the pathos in it, and collapse in a heap.

My friends called, asking what they could do. I invited them, one by one, to come over, to help me with the notes. We had had a card printed, a simple message of thanks in dark green ink with the image of a mountain on top. Still, I wanted to add a personal note on the bottom of each one. We would sit there next to each other at the dining-room table. They would write out the envelope; I would add the note. A phrase of the day typically emerged, a particular positive thought that I repeated on most of the postscripts: "We will get through this pain with the support of friends like you," or "I know Phil would want me to be happy again." Each one helped to create a vision, to point to a direction I hoped someday to be able to follow. Gradually the baskets thinned, emptied. I read each letter we had received, each note a second time, overwhelmed with gratitude for the time and care they represented.

My friend Howard, who had driven me home from the House of Prayer that horrible day, is the father of an only daughter. He wrote that because I had lost Phil, I would "never be able to be hurt that way again." Therefore, he said, I would become a "fearless warrior." At the same time, he wrote, I had been broken, in spirit and in body, broken *open*, so that I would become "both a fearless warrior and a broken open lover of the world." I thought long and hard over that one. I could see the power that could come of that. I held to the words, wanting to believe them.

Garland Wright, the Guthrie Theater's director, wrote to me: "Know this," he said at the end: "that you are loved." The letters told me of that love over and over, which filled me with hope, every day.

One night, I was home alone. I sat at the dinner table looking out at the lake. I could feel the ball of pain in my stomach, the knot in my throat, but I was dulled, frozen, unable to let it come out. My mind drifted back a couple of weeks to the tape Nicole had played in the car that day, Marc Cohn's "True Companion." Someone—Nicole or Heidi—had sent me a copy of the CD. I shuddered. Music was utterly forbidden in this new life I led. Music forced me down to a bubbling underground spring, a hot pool that I feared to tap. I pushed the thought away, but it kept coming back. I turned on the stereo and slipped the compact disc into its slot. I let the guitar, the haunting lyrics wash over me. Soon, like a volcano erupting, the ball in the pit of my stomach began to melt, became hot lava, and poured out in a torrent of tears. I held nothing back, for no one was around. I cried as I had not done since the very first day, reaching all the way down to where the pain had been born, giving in to the power of the grief, letting every ounce of it go.

When the song was over, I was limp, exhausted, spent. But then, into the vacuum, into the emptiness, rushed a surprise burst of energy. I stood up from the table and went downstairs into the room Phil had used when he came through in June on his way to Mount Rainier. I opened dresser drawers, and in them I found torn T-shirts and stained rugby shorts. I clutched them to me, buried my nose in them, but they smelled of mildew, not of Phil. I put those in a plastic bag to throw away. I found a biking jacket, which I kept to wear myself. I found a box of his books from Bates, reference sources he had used to write his thesis, books on environmentalism and spirituality. Those I set aside to give to the House of Prayer. I found photos of a camping trip he had taken with Nicole. She had shown me her set of the photographs when she was here, but she had tactfully left two of them out. One was a frontal picture of Phil, naked; the other—taken with a timer—was of the two of them walking naked away from the camera, hand in hand, toward a lake. I stared at his naked body, the body of a man, not a boy, a sight I had not seen for years. That photo was a gift I would treasure. I found a stash of letters and cards that he had saved—from me, his grandmother, his father and sisters. I decided to return these to the people who wrote them. I found a journal he had kept during a NOLS trip and continued back at school, but I couldn't bear to read it just yet.

I emptied the boxes, made piles of each thing either to save or give away. I sat back, astounded. I could not believe I had found the energy and the courage to do it all. I could see clearly then that the moving forward, the small project I had just completed, was a function of the expression of pain. Somehow the music, the tears, the emptying had created space, power, and energy to heal. I knew I would not forget this moment, one that held the key to recovery no matter how far in the future it might be.

I was reading sporadically from a book that the bishop had just given to me, a book of short meditations from John of the Cross. It was the perfect gift, for I knew I needed to explore more deeply the writings of this man whom I had come to understand in a different way, but the chapter I had just read was troubling. God wounds us, he wrote, in order to turn our eyes and hearts away from "this corrupt, dying world." He wants to teach us a lesson about investing ourselves in earthly things, in things that are not eternal. I was repulsed reading those words. I had been fighting with every fiber of my being against the notion that God is a deliberately scheming, punishing force.

A friend had sent me an article written by the Reverend William Sloane Coffin, based on a sermon he had delivered not long after his own son was killed when his car went off a road and into a river. Coffin too had struggled with this theological dilemma, and he wrote elegantly and movingly about how he had come to view it: "God's heart was the first one to break when the waves closed over my son's sinking car." Those words comforted me. We are creatures of free will, prone to misconduct, to carelessness, to accident. We are subject to the vicissitudes of weather and the actions of others. God is not the cause, but rather the well of love into which we can reach when tragedy strikes.

I knew John of the Cross was right. Everything in this world is fleeting, temporary, subject to change. I knew that we are steeped in folly, far from perfect, selfish and grounded in egotistical desires. But I was also convinced that the things we love and cherish here on earth shine so brightly *because* of their brevity, because of their tentative hold. The possibility of loss renders everything we love so precious, the very depth of the grief a function of the intensity of the love we had known. Phil's death did not mean I should not love, should not cherish, should not let myself become attached to earthly things. I only needed always to remember how vulnerable we are, how the present moment is all that we have.

Finally, I dreamed about Phil. We were together again, and the weather turned bad, a phrase I had used many times in telling the story of the accident on Mount Rainier. The weather was so bad that school was canceled. So Phil took off, playing with friends, out of sight. But then the day took a turn for the better, becoming gorgeous. There he was, off larking on this amazing day. I began looking for him, calling him back: "The weather's nice again; school is on; you must go." But he kept eluding me, slipping away, resisting. He wouldn't come back and go to school.

I woke, oddly comforted. Phil was off somewhere, cavorting in the sunshine, having a wonderful time.

CHAPTER 15

Looking for Answers

The first step in claiming yourself is anger.

Jamaica Kincaid

Summer was clearly over. For the last fifteen years, we had divided our lives between our house in the city and summers on a big lake about twenty miles west of Minneapolis. The land we had built on had belonged to Angus's parents. He had spent his childhood summers there, in a rambling, old-fashioned summer house. When we first married, I had resisted the notion of such an annual move. Though many of our friends had summer cabins in northern Minnesota, I thought that having one so close was superfluous. Angus, however, had prevailed. He had been unable to give up the land he had grown up on, where his soul was clearly rooted. Over the years, I too had come to love the new rhythm of the year. It stretched out the annual cycle; the change of scene made the months last longer. By moving altogether, we avoided our friends' weekly stress of packing, shopping, and driving hours to a cabin.

This year, we stayed three weeks longer. We needed the peace and isolation the country afforded. Toward the end of September, though, we faced the fact that the time had come to return to the city. A distinct chill hung in the air; the light had faded. The maples in our woods burst into flame. We cranked the windows tightly shut one Sunday afternoon, emptied the cupboards and the refrigerator, loaded our clothes and the dog into the car, and drove out of the driveway past the marsh, leaving the garden and the vast expanse of water behind.

I dreaded the return. Our house at the lake had been the setting of Phil's death. His absence had become a looming presence there. The support we had received, the flowers, the letters, the visits, were identified with that place and now had to be left behind. Somehow in that summer setting, with its relaxed atmosphere, its lazier pace, we had forgiven ourselves for inactivity, the lack of productivity. We had felt we had permission to mourn and to sacrifice everything to it.

Now, in returning to the city, I worried that that permission would be summarily withdrawn. Would we be expected to return to normal? Leave Phil's death behind with the few ripe tomatoes dangling on the vine, the dahlias that draped wearily over their supports? Even though scarcely more than a month had passed, would our friends expect us to be over it?

The process of moving was always tiring, but this time, with our depleted energy, it had been utterly exhausting. We drove into the garage off the alley and began unloading the cargo, making trip after trip to the closets, returning the clothes on their hangers to the places we had taken them from four months before. I made my way to the kitchen and opened the back door. On the doorstep was a basket from my friend Laura, containing homemade soup chock full of vegetables from the farmer's market, fresh bread, and a note. "You must be tired from the move," it said. "I hope this will make it easier."

The first few days in town, I was on edge, irritable. Adjusting was hard as if we had to break the news to the house, to go to each nook and cranny and see it now, for the first time, without Phil. His room had been virtually untouched since high school, his music, his books, his sports equipment. His jackets hung in several closets, his mittens and hats littered the shelves. Everywhere we turned were reminders, vestiges of a life that had suddenly, without warning, come to an end.

Late in that week after we arrived back in town, I went to my first important meeting at Hungry Mind Press, a pre-sales meeting in which we were to present our next season of books to key people in our distributors' sales force. I had barely been near the office since the accident. Though we had begun our editorial process earlier in the summer, I hadn't even read the four books my partners had finally decided to publish. I sat on the sidelines while my partners did all the presenting. I felt out of it, useless, like dead weight. I was used to being on top of things, part of the inner circle. I liked to be well-prepared. I left the meeting feeling robbed. Why now, in our second year of operation, when I was just feeling at home in the business, should I have to take a back seat, be made to look like a bystander?

I sat in the car and headed home. As I climbed the ramp and headed west on I -94, I felt rage bubbling up. Behind the wheel of my Jeep, alone in the car, I began yelling, crying, pounding the wheel, screaming at Phil. He, after all, had caused all this by dying. My exhaustion, embarrassment, and unproductivity were *his* fault. "How *dare* you do this to me?" I shouted. My voice was guttural, inhuman. "You've ruined my life! You've got to be crazy going up a mountain in the middle of the night! After all I've done for you, you don't even care about your mother, you don't think about me, you just go ahead and live your selfish, risky life the way you want to. Is this what I get for all the years of love and support I've given you?" With every breath, every pause in the screaming, a new wave of resentment and fury would come over me, a new reason that I had been so mistreated, so unappreciated, so abandoned by my ungrateful son. My voice was getting hoarse; my throat ached. Now and then I would glance at the cars around me, realize I was creating a scene, but I didn't care.

Home at last, I slammed the car door and ran into our bedroom, throwing myself on the bed, pounding the pillow like a child having a tantrum. In the midst of my wails, the phone rang. Nancy, calling from the Mayo clinic in Rochester, was hooked up to a chemotherapy machine, bored, looking for conversation. I began sobbing again, showing my oldest, dearest friend all the anger in my heart. I started at the beginning and repeated it all, let her in on every ugly, outrageous thought I had had. I knew I was safe with her. She had known me too long and too well for any surprises. I knew she would love me when I was finished, no matter how hideous a face I turned her way.

She listened patiently. She echoed my words, repeated my feelings back to me. She understood. She was a mother herself after all. She knew this place of fury. After what seemed like hours, when I was calming down, beginning to breathe easier, she sighed. "Good for you, Margaret," she said. "Now you won't get cancer."

When the episode was all over, I was exhausted, spent. In the wake of the anger, I felt shocked and sickened. Where had this come from, this incredible outpouring? I didn't really feel this way about my son, the person I had loved most in the world, did I? He had been pursuing his dreams, bravely climbing to rescue a total stranger, betrayed by faulty equipment and horrible weather. How could I be so selfish and cruel?

In reading through the books we had been given on death, many of them mentioned anger as one of the hallmarks of the grieving process. I had taken that seriously and thought long and hard about it. At whom would I be mad? God? I had wrestled with that and ultimately rejected the notion that Phil had been deliberately punished, singled out to die. John Craven, the man with the broken ankle? I had considered the possibility, but I knew he was truly a victim himself, that Phil could easily have been in John Craven's position. The Conservation Association for giving Phil the job? But it was his dream job, one he had lusted after, been thrilled to have. The Park Service? Many urged us to blame the rangers for assigning Phil to go on the rescue mission, but I knew in my heart that he had probably begged to go that night, that he had undoubtedly viewed it as the chance of a lifetime.

So here it was at last, the anger I had not been able to find, pouring from a vein that, when mined, went back to grocery store confrontations, refusals to wear winter boots, goofing off in class, high-school beer drinking. The anger was a power thing, the undeniable fact that my child had been—had always been—essentially out of my control. I was finally learning the lesson now, the hard way.

As the days began to shorten into September, Angus and I decided we had some unfinished business, some parts of Phil's life we wanted to touch personally, questions we wanted answered. We wanted to go to Bates, to meet his advisor and to hear the story of his final semester from the man who had been closest to him. We wanted to meet Sean Ryan's parents, as well as Nicole's. And we needed to visit Mount Rainier, to see whether we could come any closer to understanding what happened on that mountain, and to try to make peace with it.

Angus and I flew to Maine with a stop in New York City. We had agreed to meet the Ryans at a small Italian restaurant on the East Side. I was nervous. We still didn't know what happened that night on the mountain. We assumed that—like us—Judy and Bill were tortured by their own mental tapes, trying to conjure that icy midnight scenario. I carried a nugget of worry that they might blame Phil for what had happened, that perhaps the two of them had laid claim to the version of the story in which Phil fell first and pulled Sean over the edge. Likewise, I was curious to see whether meeting them would bring out some anger in me, whether deep down I was convinced that Sean was the culprit and that I would discover my anger in the company of his parents.

Judy is blond, athletic, full of energy. She seemed like a kindred soul, someone who could have been my friend if we lived in the same community. Bill looked strikingly like the picture of Sean in the *New York Times*. He was quiet and warm, and he glanced at me shyly out of the corner of his eye, just as Sean had in the picture.

The four of us leaned into the small table, animated and engaged, for three hours. We compared notes on Phil and Sean, learned how alike the young men had been, how they shared basic values and a passion for wild things, a love of adventure. Most of all, we felt safe, understood. We were in the presence of two people who knew exactly what we had been experiencing: the shock, the disbelief, the pain, the hopelessness, the wariness of social interaction, the fear of what the rest of our lives would hold. By the end of the evening, clearly no blame lay on either side. Any scenario could have been the truth. The boys were roped together. An accident happened, and they fell as one. When dinner ended, we vowed to keep in touch, to sustain the relationship in the years to come.

The president of Bates College had called us to offer his condolences shortly after Phil was killed. A couple of weeks later, we received a letter, saying that the college wanted to hold a memorial service in his honor and asking about a couple of proposed dates. We had agreed on a Saturday afternoon in late September.

Nicole's family owned a summer house in Maine, not far from Bates. They had invited us all—Angus and me, Todd, and my parents—to stay with them there when we came for the memorial service. When we arrived the next afternoon, we found that so many of Phil and Nicole's friends and family were coming that they had been given use of a friend's house for the occasion, to expand the available space. We settled in to a rambling cottage with views of the shore, an expanse of sand at low tide, and a tiny island off the point.

Nicole's parents were warm, friendly, and welcoming just as Phil had described them after his several visits to this same Maine retreat. I fantasized that this could have been a wedding some day, this gathering of families and friends. Instead, we were there to mourn together.

We had a clambake in local style: A huge pot filled with lobster and corn on the cob bubbled on an outdoor fire on the deck. Nicole's friends had spent the day digging clams, and we ate those dished out of another big pot on the stove. Phil's friends were there, many of the same ones from Bates who had made the trip to Minnesota. Stew and Dryw and another Minnesota friend came up from New York.

As we sat finishing dinner, a Bates classmate named Alix burst into the room, flushed with excitement. She held piles of books and photographs in her arms. They had been able to stop the presses on the Bates 1995 yearbook and they added a final page inside the back cover dedicated to Phil. Alix had still more of a surprise. Amazingly, her senior project for a course in photography that year had been a photographic portrait of Phil. Alix had literally dozens of artful black-and-white photographs of him, none of which I had ever seen. There were shots with friends, on the rugby field, with Nicole, in casual settings on the campus. She had mounted a set of the best in her studio and printed them on acid-free paper, to display the next day at the Bates service. Best of all, she said we could take them home. We spent a long time over the pictures, laughing and crying, hearing stories about life at Bates. At last, exhausted, we retired to our little room listening to the rain pound the windows and the wind howl.

We were sitting, Angus, Todd, and I, at a table in a restaurant near the Bates campus with Carl Straub, professor of religion and environmental studies. I had been so eager to meet this man who was Phil's thesis advisor. Phil had admired and trusted him, and I wanted to know him too, to learn the process by which *"Consider the Lilies"* came to be. Carl had written us a lovely, personal letter upon learning about Phil's death, and I called him to set up this meeting when we knew we were coming to Bates.

Carl was bigger than I thought he would be; he was tall, somewhat jowly, professorial. I had pictured a shy man, but Carl was comfortable, self-confident, a strong presence. I was thinking, as I ate my tuna sandwich, that I could easily see why Phil admired him, why he liked and trusted him. I could also understand why Phil grew nervous before their regular meetings. Carl was not someone who would tolerate slackers easily.

We had come because we wanted to solve the mystery of Phil's final performance. How had this usually average student, raised in a secular household, come to write a lyrical, fascinating thesis on Christian environmentalism that had earned an A? Was Carl a strong, guiding force? Had he suggested organization, sources, directions for Phil's cogent arguments? More important, had Carl inspired Phil's interest in Christianity? Had his careful editing produced the engaging prose that was a hallmark of the piece? I was searching his face, wondering these things, when Carl leaned forward over the table.

No, he insisted. He had not conceived, written, or organized the paper. He knew, he added, that Phil's love of nature and adventure was longstanding, entrenched, born of experience. "But where," he asked earnestly, "did Phil's lyrical Christian imagery come from? Do you have a family history of Christian practice?" We laughed, shook our heads, and wondered together at the mystery, the grace that led to Phil's final academic act.

We settled into seats in the front of the Bates College chapel and watched students and faculty members file in slowly behind us. Who were they and why were they here on a brilliant fall Saturday? Phil's class had already graduated. Could all of these people have known him?

Nicole was seated nearby. I knew she had prepared something to read, but I couldn't believe she would actually be able to do it. She knew without a doubt, she had told me that morning, that Phil would have spoken for her had it been the other way around.

At last I saw her stand, approach the microphone. The paper was steady in her hand. Her voice was strong and sure. In this "wordless moment," she urged us to look for Phil in the world around us:

> Go lie by a brook on a tract of grass. Feel the earth breathe beneath you as you breathe. Find the water currents that flow through you. . . . In that moment of interconnectedness, you will be with Phil.

> Laugh, really laugh. If that laughter comes from the heart, Phil's laughter will resound through you.

> Let the mountain goats lead you up nameless ridges and peaks. Listen to the mountain's stories. When you reach the summit, Phil will be waiting there.

> Love someone, not because of the love you expect in return but because you are not afraid.

CHAPTER 16

Terrible Glory

What becomes
of the past if the future
snaps off, brittle,
the present left as a jagged edge
opening on nothing?

Denise Levertov

On the way from Maine to Mount Rainier, we made a stop in the California wine country. Some Minneapolis friends had offered to let us use their weekend house in the Sonoma Valley for several days. Angus and I had fallen in love with that area over the past ten years or so, spending weekends in the adjacent Napa Valley each time we traveled to California for his twice-yearly meetings of the Stanford Business School board. The previous spring we had found a piece of property we were in the process of buying, so we were eager to spend time there, to get away from home, and to resume our dreams of the future that had just been so cruelly interrupted.

The weather in the wine country at the end of September was glorious. We would wake slowly, urged into consciousness by the ruddy glow of a sunrise coming through the French doors of our friends' bedroom. We ate our meals on a wide expanse of terrace overlooking their olive orchard. We read, wrote notes, and walked, exploring the hilly, winding roads nearby that wandered under arching branches of live oaks hung with sage green moss, past acres of grapevines turning vibrant shades of red and yellow. We ate heirloom tomatoes, ripe from local vines, crusty bakery bread slathered with overripe cheeses, and washed it all down with icy chardonnay.

On occasion, I could almost forget. We knew no people here, so we had no one to meet and greet. Here, we were no longer tragic figures who loomed in everyone's daily thoughts. We were not pitied, worried over, guiltily avoided. We could grieve alone, in private, at our own pace, and I found that the sadness became a more natural, mellow presence, rather like the afterglow of a robust cabernet. One day, at five o'clock on our afternoon walk, I turned to Angus in shock. "Do you realize I have not cried yet, not once today?" Forty-eight days had passed since Phil's death. I counted. I didn't make it to bedtime without tears, but it was just the idea—the hope, really—that had for the first time let itself be touched and felt.

At the end of the week, we flew north to Seattle into the shadow of Mount Rainier. Heidi and Andrew were with us. Chris flew in from Boulder and met us there. The first night, we had dinner as a family at a small French restaurant, a cozy room with flowered wallpaper and botanical prints on the walls. We sat at the table and spun out fantasies of a future life with a place in the wine country. We played with possible names for the vineyard. As I sat there listening to the laughter the chatter, an unbearable loneliness settled over me.

Here was the only family I had, but I was utterly alone within it. My friend, my own son, my ally was gone. Here were Angus and his three children, *his* family. I was an interloper, an outsider. I didn't belong. I felt my throat begin to swell, and I excused myself from the table, headed quietly for the bathroom. As I leaned my head against the cold tiled wall, letting myself give in to the grief, the door opened gently. Heidi had sensed my pain and followed me.

I felt ugly. My face was distorted, my nose and eyes streaming, but I looked at her squarely, unflinchingly. I told her exactly what it was all about: my sense of alienation, the loneliness. She studied me, listening. Then she shook her head. "You're right," she said. "You two *were* a team. But don't you see?"

"See what?" I said, searching her face, not understanding.

"Now, in his absence, we can be closer to you," she answered, "more than ever before." She hugged me, comforted me. Out of the ashes, a blessing.

It is early, very early the next morning. There is a steady drizzle, but it hasn't stopped us. We are in the car, according to plan. We have come on a pilgrimage, a complicated mission. We have with us a small bag with the remainder of Phil's ashes. We've set out to make friends with this place that Phil loved, to confront this mountain that has robbed us of so much.

I am on edge, as if a lump hiding just below the swallow line threatens at any moment to ride up my throat and explode. Two hours on the road . . . even in the rain the colorful changing leaves are beautiful. It is autumn, a time of endings, of letting go. The road narrows. We cannot see Mount Rainier for the clouds, but we know it is there, pulling us on, as if we have hitched the car to a giant winch, and there is no way to turn back. At last, we confront a huge timbered entrance gate lettered simply "Mount Rainier National Park." We drive under it, and I draw a deep breath. Here. His place.

We follow signs to the White River Ranger Station, the address I have sent so much mail to all summer long, and pull alongside the ticket taker. "Five dollars, please," she says. Five dollars. We hand over the money, and I think, You can't imagine the price we have really paid to be here.

Mike Gauthier, the head climbing ranger, Phil's roommate and mentor during his summer there, was waiting for us inside the ranger station. He was even handsomer than I remembered from our brief encounter in Minneapolis for Phil's funeral—tall, dark, and energized, a smile always at his lips. His nose was finely chiseled, his lower jaw ever so slightly undercast, giving him an approachable, gentle demeanor. He was glad to see us, and right away he began tracing Phil's last route for us on big wall posters of the mountain. "Here is Camp Schurman," he said, "where they got the call." Then his finger moved up, up, showing us how amazingly far they traveled that night, until they were only two hundred feet from their destination. ". . . And here is where they fell." It looked so far, so cold. He told us the story of his own rescue mission the next morning, how they had backed the helicopter in, how they ran to the boys, how they knew right away that they were dead. *Poor Mike*, I thought. *How hard to lose two friends like that, how hard to have to find their bodies.*

We pulled on our rain gear for the trek up to Phil's campsite at Glacier Basin. It was pouring by then, a steady rain. We hiked up the trail, a former logging road, lined on both sides with tall, handsome trees that opened now and then on the left to a deep ravine. Waterfalls appeared at regular intervals, berries, wildflowers, turning leaves. I walked up front with Mike. The trek was a climb all the way, but not too steep, and we kept up a steady patter. I wanted to hear his story of that terrible night, his version of what happened. He mentioned that the rope between Phil and Sean had been too long, which probably made it harder for the remaining climber to arrest the other. He said they had found Phil's ice axe stuck in the ice up where they had stopped, his wrist strap left unattached, something a climber should never do. I asked him about Phil's broken crampon, something that had been nagging at the back of my brain. "Everyone has crampon problems," he said. "I had them last week, Sean the week before Phil."

But still, he wondered, had they trained Phil carefully enough, given him enough instruction on how to adjust them properly? Maybe the fall had happened when they were adjusting Phil's crampon. He mentioned Sean's gloveless hand, the unzipped backpack. Maybe it had happened when Sean was reaching for the radio. "In any case," he said, "it was cold and icy. They slipped. That is all we will ever know."

At last, drenched and cold, we arrived at Glacier Basin, at the rangers' campsite, and it was just as Phil had so lovingly described it: a vast, long meadow, a mountain lake nestled under glaciers rising on all sides. The lupine was mostly gone by then, faded away, but I could imagine what it must have been like when it was laid with a brilliant carpet of blue. I could see him sitting there, counting deer, dreaming of climbing to the sky.

We worked our way down into the meadow, retrieved the bag of ashes, and poured them into some paper cups we had brought along. I dipped my hand in, rubbing the grainy texture between my fingertips, greedily filling my fist. "I love you, Phil. This is a beautiful place, and it is right to leave you here." I raised my arm, let the ashes go, and the wind took hold, dusting them in a fine arc lightly over the faded lupine at my feet. I watched the particles settle, washing into the crevices of blossom. I wanted to remember this, the last time I would touch my son. The others did the same, each walking off to accomplish this last parting in a solitary part of the meadow.

"I think that Phil would want us to have a party now," I said at last. It was cold. We shivered, eating our terrible convenience-store sandwiches quickly, gulping down too much candy, hoping the sugar would keep us warm. On the way down, the sun came out. We stopped now and then, looking back at the shifting clouds, hoping to catch a glimpse of the summit, the mountain that we knew was there and could not see. But it was hidden, determined to stay out of reach.

The landing gear groans as our early morning plane takes off, banking sharply to head east for home. I have still not yet been face-to-face with Mount Rainier. I glance down out of the window, and my heart stops. There it is, huge, gleaming white above the clouds, defiant in all of its terrible glory.

CHAPTER 17

Continental Divide

You do not honor the dead by dying with them.

Ingrid Trobisch

On a brilliant October day a couple of weeks after our return from Mount Rainier, I was walking the three-mile path that winds around the small lake near our house in the city. The air was brisk, the sun warm against my face. Leaves were swirling at my feet; a slight breeze ruffled my hair. This kind of day used to fill my soul with joy, and I missed joy. I was beginning to long for it. I walked slowly. Then, gradually, the landscape gave way beneath my feet. I was no longer walking on flat ground but along a narrow path among the clouds. I felt as if I were hiking the Continental Divide. The view from up there was awesome, and I felt a sudden surge of freedom.

That morning I had read an article sent to me by an old friend from high school. The author was a college religion professor, who described a family car accident in which he had lost—all at once—his mother, his wife, and a daughter. Overwhelmed with grief, he still had two other children who needed his love and attention. Like Job, he said, in the face of such disaster, we are confronted with a terrifying yet undeniable freedom: the freedom to choose how we respond. The death of a loved one happens *to* us, he wrote. But then comes the possibility of another death: our own, the death of the spirit. We can decide whether or not we will compound the tragedy with yet another loss, giving death the upper hand.

I had been paging through old journals that morning when my eye had fallen on a passage written a few days after Christmas three years before. Two of Phil's soccer teammates had died tragically in a car accident on Christmas Eve that year. After attending the funeral of one of them, Phil came home in tears. He was in college then and tears were rare. I held him, his shoulders wide like a man's, rubbed his back, let him cry. "Oh Phil," I said, "I'm so sorry about your friend."

"I'm not crying about him, Mom," he said. "I'm crying about *you*."

I held my breath. "Me?"

"He was his mom's only child, just like I am. I was watching her during the service, and all I could think of was you. What would happen to you if anything ever happened to me?"

I stared at the journal passage, riveted to the words. I had forgotten all about the encounter. Did he have some premonition of his own death, one of those rare glimpses out of time and space? It seemed that way. But what really mattered was the clear message the words held. Phil's pain then was for me, now. Phil loved life; he cherished it. The worst thing he could imagine, an image that reduced him to sobs, was of a mother—*his* mother—grieving, sad, destroyed by the death of her son. Suddenly, on that October day, I knew with certainty that Phil would want me to be happy, to be the Mom he knew and loved. He would *hate* this, the fact that he died. He would be kicking himself, pissed off that he blew it, that they could have slipped like that, that he and Sean could have really, actually *died*. He would be watching me from wherever he was, anxiously wringing his hands, holding his breath. Will she make it? Will she be OK? What can I do to make her feel better, to help her over this painful, hideous grief?

I knew that I owed it to him to recover, to go on to live life to the fullest, for both of us. I suddenly saw that I had a choice: to crumple under the weight of the pain or to take the latent energy of this explosion in the middle of my life and harness it, turn it outward into love, compassion, and creativity. I couldn't imagine how, for I could feel only pain and grief. But suddenly I had been offered a vision, a goal, one that I knew Phil would endorse, one that I could turn to for direction.

As I continued along that Continental Divide, I began to feel that Phil was walking beside me, holding my hand, leading me forward. I knew then that he would be the one to give me the strength to say no to the death of the spirit, he would help me to resist the pull of pain, to deflect the anger. I owed it to my son, who had been deprived of so much of his life. When I was pregnant, people said I was "eating for two." Now I knew that I was *living* for two. I had a new challenge, a new responsibility, as if Phil were inside me again, offering me an opportunity: a double dose of energy, curiosity, and purpose. But how could I possibly rise to the occasion? How could I find the strength to meet the challenge?

Now that I had no biological children of my own, I began to think about the importance of my own family of origin. My parents had always been central in my life, but they would not be around forever. I began to consider my sister Martha and her family in a new light. With all of the confusion following Phil's death, the two of us had not yet had a chance to sit down together and talk one-on-one. Her birthday was the second week in October, and I called her to arrange a meeting at a restaurant in our neighborhood. I would buy her lunch to celebrate.

I am the firstborn of two, older than Martha by four years. Growing up, we were often at odds. I was the big sister, always ahead, always in charge. We played together and fought like all sisters do, but as the years passed, the differences between us became more and more pronounced. I was the student, she the artist. I was conventional, predictable; she was nonconformist, even rebellious at times. I went to Smith and wore plaid skirts and penny loafers; she went to Bennington and became something of a flower child.

As adults we have compared notes on our upbringing, and I have often been amazed. We seemed to be raised in two completely different families. I thrived on the praise I received and thought I deserved. I felt encouraged, supported, cheered. In the same household, with the same parents, she remembers being surrounded by anger and disappointment, felt she was unappreciated and judged. She spent years in therapy in a deliberate effort to sort out these influences. She became a psychologist herself, educated and inspired by her own quest for understanding. In Phil's first few years, she was a dedicated aunt, taking him for hours at a time when I, separated and a single parent, needed time alone. She loved Phil, and she was eager to share her accumulated experience as a daughter, her growing store of knowledge of child psychology. But, as usual, we did not always see eye to eye.

Once, when Phil was about six, she was at our house for dinner. I picked my son up and held him on my lap, nuzzling him on the neck. "You shouldn't kiss him so much," she said. "He'll feel smothered." I was irritated, resentful. She was not a mother herself. How dare she try to tell me how to parent? We settled into a kind of respectful distance. We eagerly joined together as an extended family on holidays, but she and I had only occasional interaction, just the two of us. I had the sense that our history had left a store of resentment that she was in no hurry to overcome.

When she married in her mid-thirties, I couldn't wait to see how this would all play out, how she would be as a parent herself. I watched with fascination, skepticism, and wonder. When she was pregnant, Martha blossomed into an earth mother. Hardly a book on pregnancy or childbirth was printed that she did not devour. The boys slept in small cribs at the foot of their parents' bed for many months. As babies, they were seldom allowed to cry. At any hour of the day or night, if so much as a whimper would emerge, either she or her husband would drop everything to find the cause. They seemed to have no particular feeding schedule but would be nursed on demand at any hour, in any setting. Martha nursed each of the older two almost until the next was born (two years, then three) and her third son until he was nearly five.

Babysitters were mature and carefully screened in their household. Wherever the parents went, often their children went too. In the early years, they preferred to stay home with the boys rather than go out to see a concert or go to dinner parties. They chose friends of a like mind and often did things together with the children included. Eventually one of my sister's friends from high school became a favorite sitter; they used her almost exclusively. A postponed honeymoon to Europe was dropped indefinitely; as the children grew, they never left them to travel alone together until the oldest was fourteen. They sent their boys to a Waldorf school, where the toys were of natural materials, the rooms draped in pastel muslin, the passage of the seasons marked with ritual storytelling and candles.

I had made different choices. Phil had always slept in his own room in a separate bed down the hall. I nursed him for ten months, then switched him right to a cup. I had left him easily with young neighborhood sitters since the beginning and followed the "twenty minute rule": if he cried some night when I put him to sleep, I wouldn't pick him up for twenty minutes on the theory that he was just fussy, exhausted. That approach always seemed to work long before the twenty minutes expired. I took on a part-time job when

Phil was two, worked full-time from the time he was four. We sent him to public, then conventional independent schools. Angus and I traveled often, occasionally for three weeks at a time.

I watched my sister with fascination in light of these differences. I was skeptical, critical—just as she had been with me—but no one could deny the proof that was in the pudding. Phil was a wonderful boy; I had no regrets. On her end, Martha was raising three exceptionally interesting and nice children.

In early September, a month after Phil died, we gathered as a family to celebrate our father's seventy-fourth birthday. My parents hosted the lunch for Angus and me, my sister and her husband and the three boys. Her oldest, a gentle, sensitive boy of eleven, was excited about origami paper folding and struggling with an attempt to learn to knit. I was astounded at his solid core, his quiet determination and self-confidence around adults. The second, hardy and athletic, was earnestly poring over a book on tractors, full of energy and curiosity. Her youngest was—as usual—delighting us all with his precocious vocabulary and the devilish glint in his eye. As we finished lunch, I looked around the room. Jealousy and resentment gnawed at my stomach: these three beautiful children were alive, growing, and thriving, and my only son was dead. It wasn't just, it wasn't fair! I could hold back the tears no longer. Their normally cheerful Aunt Margaret released a flood of self-pity and grief in front of everyone and left the party for home.

Now, a month later, on her birthday, Martha and I sat facing each other across the table, just the two of us. I reached down beside me and handed her a wrapped package. She opened it and pulled out a small black leather bag with a silver zipper, designed by a woman whose jewelry I knew she loved. "Perfect." She looked up at me laughing. "You won't believe it," she said, "but I'm carrying the very same purse today!"

We took our time over steaming bowls of minestrone. I found I could talk freely and openly. She was family, after all. I could let the tears flow whenever they surfaced more comfortably than I could with my friends. I was vulnerable. The tables had turned; the balance of power in our relationship had shifted. I felt secure in her presence, and I found that I was eager to hear her insights, to bounce my own thoughts off against her wisdom. I was beginning to see that I trusted her in a way I had not previously appreciated.

She leaned across the table eagerly. "There's something I've wanted to tell you," she said, "something I learned when I was studying psychology. Each of us yearns at some primal level to be an only child, to have our parents' love all to ourselves. You should feel good, looking back, that Phil lived all his life with that security, knowing that he was your one and only, that he never had to share your parental love with anyone."

I had never thought about that before, and I found a measure of comfort in it. Phil, of course, longed on occasion for a "real" brother or sister. I was delighted at the bonds he formed with Chris, Andrew, and Heidi. But still, she had a point—she who had felt like a second fiddle for decades. My son lived twenty-two years knowing he had no rival in my eyes.

I considered my situation. One of the biggest fears and regrets at the heart of my grief was the fact that I had no children, no progeny to leave behind as my contribution to the world. My particular genes had reached a dead end. But now I looked at my sister and thought how much she looked like me. My hair was curlier, but we had the same brown eyes, the same broad face, a similar smile, nearly identical voices. She and I were products of the same parents, our DNA two random combinations of the very same genes. One half of Phil was descended from those two grandparents as was half of each of her three sons. Maybe this gene thing wasn't such a big deal after all, I thought. Maybe, in a way, my nephews could fill the progeny bill.

We left the restaurant and came outside. As I looked at her, I could feel that the air had cleared—like a summer morning after the rain. She turned to me and hugged me tight. "I love you," she said, and I could tell that she meant it.

CHAPTER 18

The Birthday Visitor

Inside this new love, die.
Your way begins on the other side.
Become the sky.
Take an axe to the prison wall.
Escape.

Rumi

Now it was my turn for a birthday. My fiftieth loomed ahead in mid-November, a huge barrier to be passed, one that was rife with issues, questions, and doubts. Arguably, fifty years marked the halfway point in my life. Both my grandmothers had lived into their mid-nineties. Allowing for improvements in healthcare and more conscious lifestyle choices, I could well live to be a hundred. How could I only be at the halfway point, when—as far as I could see—my life was over? I had nothing to look forward to; nothing but pain loomed in my future.

In July we had decided that we would celebrate my turning fifty with a huge party, inviting all our friends to a dinner and blowout night of dancing. We were clear about that one: we canceled the party long before invitations would have been sent. We had also decided that after the party, we would fly to California, rent a car, and drive down the coast, just the two of us. That aspect of the celebration was a different story. We both looked forward to going away again. We appreciated the support, but we tired of the attention and scrutiny. The idea of the two of us, alone in a car, anonymous to everyone but each other, sounded too good to be true. We decided to go ahead with the trip.

Two friends had approached me a couple of weeks earlier. Since you canceled your party, they said, would you be willing to let us give you a small birthday dinner, just a few good friends? Fifty was an important birthday, after all. I really didn't want to let it pass unacknowledged, so I agreed. The night before Angus and I left on our trip, twelve of us gathered for dinner. They had each brought part of the meal, as well as a big decorated white cake with sparklers on it. I received toasts and cards and—as if I were a child again—a pile of beautifully wrapped presents, a real, old-fashioned birthday party. As the toasts wound down, as I sat at the head of the table surrounded by torn paper and shredded ribbons, I looked around at my friends. I felt as if a wave of love had swept over me, as if I were bathed in it, held up, encircled. I tried to make a toast myself, to speak to them from my heart of how much their love meant to me. But my lips would not move. All I could do was to hold up my glass.

Angus and I were sitting at a table for two in the noisy din of Mustard's, a favorite Napa Valley restaurant, the first stop in my birthday trip down the California coast. We had just visited our new vineyard property again, and we were filled with excitement, imagining a future in which those acres of grapevines, glowing red now in the November afternoon sun, would soon mark the days of our lives with their seasonal changes and the drama of transforming their fruit into wine. As we sat there, I thought about memory and about future, and suddenly I saw Phil in a new light.

My memories of him, I realized, were no different from other parents' memories of their own living children. If I thought about him at age five, ten, or fifteen, those memories were vivid and real, but that

Phil was long gone. My friends felt the same way. Their memories of their children were vivid too, and real, but their child of five or ten years old was as gone as Phil. On the other hand, any future fantasies of Phil that I had ever had were not real, only phantom images, visions, figments of my imagination. I still had the power to imagine a future Phil, fantasize about what might have been. So those images were not lost to me. Those future fantasies were no more real for parents of living children. They at least had the possibility of a future for their child, but no guarantees, no certainty. Anything could happen. All their plans and visions were no more than products of the imagination. So what was I missing? All I had ever really had of Phil, it seemed, was the experience of the present moment, one that shifted as it passed, infinitely small, forever elusive, forever changing. *This* moment, *this* moment, *this* one now. I looked across the table into my husband's eyes, and at that very moment, my love for him was more present to me than the memories, the fantasies, even than the grief.

We loaded our bags into the car and took off. We had rented a convertible—what else could we do for a drive down the California coast?—but it was November, and a chill was in the air. We bundled up in sweaters, jackets, and even hats so we could keep the top down, and we headed first up the coast to Mendocino, then turned south toward Los Angeles. The air was clear, then foggy, then clear again. The wind was strong and steady. The waves crashed in giant white foaming geysers against the craggy rocks along the coast. We drove and talked and drove and looked and tried to stay in the present moment.

South of San Francisco, in Palo Alto, Angus had a two-day meeting to attend at Stanford Business School. I had decided to check into Mercy Center in Burlingame for two days of retreat with Father Tom Hand, David Keller's spiritual mentor. I had attended a weekend retreat he had led at the House of Prayer the previous May.

A Catholic priest, Father Hand had spent more than twenty years living in Japan studying Zen meditation. The weekend in Minnesota, a silent retreat, had been powerful for me. The twenty or so retreatants had met and chatted at dinner Friday night, but after that—other than the formal question-and-answer sessions—we had existed side by side without talking. Our meals, our breaks were taken in silence. Tom Hand was a towering presence. He was not a particularly big man physically, but he had seemed so grounded, so integrated, so still, that he loomed large. He gave fascinating lectures, and during each session of sitting meditation, he would punctuate the time periods with powerful aphorisms that echoed in my soul, often for hours.

The second night of that retreat, I sat up at two in the morning, my heart pounding, twisted in damp sheets, my neighbor from the room next to mine banging on my door, awakened by my screams. "Are you all right?" she had called out anxiously. "Are you having a nightmare?" She hugged me to her, worried for my safety. Even upon awakening, I was still engulfed in a horrible dream: I am trapped, sealed in a burial vault whose cover slid inexorably closed above my head. I am told that the only means of escape is to remember the secret language instructions I had been given, but I cannot remember. I panic. I begin banging the sides of the white rectangular vault screaming, "Help! Help! Help!"

When the weekend was finished, I was determined to study again with Father Hand, to spend more time in his presence. I had suggested then to him that perhaps I could participate in another retreat to mark my fiftieth birthday in the fall. No retreat was scheduled anywhere at that time, he had replied, but maybe I could spend a few days at Mercy Center, the convent where he lived and worked south of San Francisco. He urged me to consider it and to write to him if I still wanted to come. Little did I know then how much I would need such a visit.

As our car nosed its way up the long driveway to the entrance of the convent, I remembered my nightmare the previous May. Had it been a premonition? Had that white rectangular coffin I experienced then been a glimpse of what I now found myself engulfed in, a kind of living death from which there seemed no escape? Was I now trying to learn the secret language that would give me the keys to move out of and beyond the prison of grief in which I was trapped?

I checked in at the desk and was shown to my room. This was a far cry from the natural wood and stone of the House of Prayer. I passed through institutional, outdated spaces, down dull, dark hallways, threw my bag into a room furnished with cheap fabrics and depressing furniture. Was two nights a grave mistake, I wondered?

But then I wandered outside and began slowly to encircle the property on the Zen walking trails that Father Hand had painstakingly carved into the acreage surrounding the convent. They were lovely, carpeted in a dense ground cover. Each turn of the path would reveal a new treasure: a fallen log, a tree elegantly pruned to reveal its gnarly, unique character. The sun set slowly, its glowing colors framed by the ever-changing web of branches over my head. When I came back inside, a profound silence greeted me, my room now merely simple, without pretension, clean, undistracting. Here I can simply be, I thought.

At seven that night, I headed toward the meditation room. I was scared. Though over the past four years, I had developed a regular personal practice, it had fallen apart since Phil's death. I avoided time alone, stayed in bed in the mornings worrying, fretting, crying. The prospect of sitting for twenty minutes confronting the depths of my grief filled me with nothing but dread. I had looked at Jean Vail across a lunch table a week or so before. "I can't pray. I can't meditate anymore," I told her.

"Why not?" she asked.

"Because each time I try," I said, "I end up sitting there crying my heart out, nothing more."

"That's all right," she had said quickly. "Do it anyway. Just sit. Just cry."

But I hadn't. I hadn't even made it once through a twenty-minute period. Now I was joining a group of total strangers, expecting to make it for a couple of hours. I hesitated as I walked down the hall, ready to back out, to head to my room. I looked up and saw Father Hand, dressed in loose pants and his short Japanese wrapped jacket, one he had worn for our sessions at the House of Prayer. He recognized me, stretched his hand out warmly. "It is good to see you," he said.

The room was serene. Painted in cool, earth tones, a platform in one corner supported a Zen rock and sand garden. Shelves surrounded a Buddha and Christ in relief, objects for meditation like bells and gongs. Brown chairs and *zafu* floor cushions were arranged in a circle. With some trepidation, I settled onto a cushion and crossed my legs. The drum sounded, a piercing series of raps on a hollow gourd . . . a taped chant . . . thirty minutes of silence . . . a walking meditation . . . thirty more minutes of silence . . . a talk by Father Hand . . . thirty more minutes of sitting. I was astounded when it was over. I had made it! Moreover, the practice had been good, peaceful, and deep. My legs had not gone to sleep until the last five minutes or so. Just before we left, Father Hand beckoned to me. "How about a chat in my office, about eleven tomorrow morning?"

I woke at dawn and stumbled in the dark down to the chapel for meditation at 6:30. Lines of people were seated on cushions. Some were nuns from the convent; others were neighbors who came each morning to join the ritual. We heard again the rapping, rapping drum, then perhaps forty-five minutes of silence. When the session was over, I couldn't feel my feet, my ankles, my knees, all the way up to my hips. I lurched and grabbed the rail of the choir stall for support.

Father Hand and I met for nearly an hour in his book-lined, cluttered, comfortable office. I had written to him of Phil's death, so he knew why I had come. I told him the stories, especially the mysterious ones: the fox, the meditation the morning I found out, my early introduction to Jean Vail. None of it surprised him. He spoke of force fields, levels and categories of existence, how in meditation we transcend the individual level and are open to communication, to connection.

He reminded me that the pain of loss is essentially selfish, focused on the needs of our own ego, not the needs of the person who has died. The soul does not die, he said. It continues and is closer to us than before. As I stood to leave, he looked at me long and hard. "This death," he said. "It's part of your path." I thought of John of the Cross and nodded. He added slowly, "And it is good. Deep down it is good." I turned and walked away, not understanding, but—in an odd way—trusting.

That night he met me at seven and led me to a room where a video recorder had been placed. He had been eager for me to watch a tape called "Life After Life." The author, Raymond Moody, had interviewed over two thousand people who had had near-death experiences, people who had essentially died and lived to tell the tale. Despite the diversity in ages and backgrounds of the subjects of the interviews, they seemed to agree to an amazing extent.

In these interviews, people said they had left their bodies, floated above them. They were aware of their own bodies lying there, the people around them. They traveled through time and space, saw other people. Then they were guided into a long tunnel that ascended to a brilliant light; then they found themselves in the presence of a powerful, loving being. I remembered the story Howard had told me in the car that first day, driving home from the House of Prayer.

In the context of the all-embracing love that surrounded them, these people saw their lives displayed all at once in a panorama. They were made to see that life's major milestones of achievement were not what mattered. Instead the little spontaneous acts of love, respect, and kindness between themselves and others had counted. They saw the ripple effect of their behavior and how it had affected others. They all came back to life—reluctantly—and once back, they became more spiritual and did not fear death. The video was extraordinary, and I climbed the stairs to my little room thinking about Phil.

Indeed, his moment of death there on the mountain after the terror of the fall must have been peaceful, even ecstatic—the "white moment" he had written of, but greater still than achieving a mountain's summit. He must have floated above his body lying still on the glacier, covered with snow. It was night. Did he travel? See me sleeping in Minneapolis, Nicole in Sun Valley? I could imagine him watching the panorama of his life in intricate detail—the childhood games, the teenage parties with friends, listening to music, playing soccer, hiking with Nicole. The sad and frustrating moments too must have passed before his eyes—his parents' divorce, the fall through the ice, his clashes with teachers, his final slip and fall. Did he feel me holding him in my arms as a baby, see again and know the love I felt for him every minute? He must have felt good about his life. The loving presence must have praised him for all his many small acts of kindness, for his final thesis when he tried to wake the world up, for his last climb on Mount Rainier, for persevering toward the man with the broken ankle. Maybe he thought about coming back like those others in the video, but his body was too broken.

My vision of Phil's death was a fantastic tale. But why not? Such events had certainly been corroborated by thousands of people from varying walks of life. I could see that love was the underlying unity out of which all life comes. In my profound love for Phil, in my devoted love for Angus, I participate in love. I claim it, make it part of me. The love never dies. If the object of love is absent, the love is not diminished. It is still part of me, still defines me, still drives me. So in loving others—small gestures, loyal support, generous acts, open communion—I stay alive; I honor Phil; I manifest the love of God. I drifted off to sleep, calmed and less afraid of dying.

Angus was there at the doorstep in the morning after my last turn on the walking paths. I jumped into the convertible and we were off down the coast: Monterey, Big Sur, San Simeon, Morro Bay. We took pictures of each other, walked on stony beaches, watched for whales. We had romantic lunches on seaside terraces, hiked through forested hills, slept in picturesque inns. On the night before my birthday, the two of us checked in to Mount Calvary, an Episcopal monastery of the order of the Holy Cross, high in the hills overlooking Santa Barbara. The monastery was an old Spanish hacienda with stunning views, a red tile roof, glowing dark wood floors that creaked, French doors opening onto flowered terraces, timbered beams in the ceiling, and a calm, quiet atmosphere. This is what we want our new house in the Napa Valley to feel like, I thought.

It is the day I turn fifty. It is dawn in the Santa Barbara monastery, and I have just made a trip to the bathroom. I slip back into bed and lie there quietly, holding Angus's hand. Right away, it seems—so soon that I cannot have fallen asleep—I am pushing a wheelchair through a hall somewhere. In the chair, covered with a blanket, is Phil's body. I turn briefly away, but someone says, "Look! The blanket is moving!" I lift it, and there is Phil, totally alive and well. The vision is so clear, so real, not like a dream at all. He looks and sounds exactly as he always has. He is healthy, healed; he looks great. I ask him what he is doing here. "I wasn't ready to die," he said. "So I came back." I ask him if he has seen Nicole, and he replies yes, many times. I ask him if he has seen me crying. "Oh no," he says. "I can't bear to. It is too horrible, too sad." He puts his hand through a wall in a ghostly way to show me that he is all spirit now. I am about to ask him exactly what happened to him and Sean, but I open my eyes and find myself in the monastery in the bed next to Angus. At first, I am convinced it was not a dream. Phil is, in fact, alive again. I wake Angus excitedly to tell him about it, but as I talk, it fades, ripples out into shadow.

We hiked into the hills that morning, then moved from the peace of the monastery to our final weekend at a Santa Barbara inn. A vase of flowers was waiting in our room from my parents and a bottle of champagne sent by Jean Vail. We celebrated there, a delicious birthday dinner with a bottle of good wine. Angus gave me a pearl and white gold brooch that was a dangling bunch of grapes, symbolic of our future together in the Napa Valley. But as I drifted off to sleep that night, what comforted me, what excited me, was the birthday visit from Phil.

CHAPTER 19

First Christmas

Aren't there annunciations
of one sort or another
in most lives?

Denise Levertov

As we settled back into Minnesota after our weeks in California, the air turned frigid. We dragged boots, hats, and mittens from closets, pulled the storm windows in tight and waited for snow. Looking ahead, I could see nothing but the big hole that loomed before us: Christmas.

I had always been a holiday person. Every year in November and December, my birthday, Thanksgiving, and Christmas followed closely upon each other, and I looked forward to the season. I relished it and would celebrate for six weeks running. Like a child, I loved the anticipation, the music, the decorations, the gift giving, the family gatherings. I entered into all of it with enthusiasm and joy. Now a sense of dread settled upon me.

I could feel the relapse in my bones. In yoga class in early December, we spent a morning practicing backbends. I have learned in studying this Eastern discipline that we commonly hold our emotions, the feelings that lodge in our hearts, tightly in a contracted chest. We slump, round our shoulders, thrust our neck and chin forward to form a sort of protective hollow around our hearts. Backbends open us up. They force the sternum out, thrust it upward. They pry the ribs apart, crack open and expose the heart to the world. In the third half-hour of class that morning, I positioned my hands on the rubber mat, bent my knees and pushed upward into a backbend.

In a flash I see Phil in my mind's eye, far away down the concourse at the airport, his silhouette unmistakable in the Christmas crowd gathered at the baggage carousel. His baseball hat is on backward, the tufts of blond hair sticking out over his ears. He is dressed in an oversized red parka, hoisting a duffel bag over his shoulder. As I run toward him, he turns, sees me, smiles his inimitable smile. "Hi Mom!" he says, opening his arms. "It's great to be home."

I couldn't breathe. I felt a wave of nausea and pain rise from my stomach into my chest and lodge in a scream, stuck in my throat. I dropped back down to the yoga mat, put my hand over my mouth, ran from the room and hid in the bathroom, sobbing guttural sobs as if I would turn inside out.

I left class early and drove to the cemetery, several blocks away. I stood in front of Phil's grave, the granite slab covered with a thin layer of snow. Hundreds of bird footprints were all over it. I sat for minutes, maybe half an hour in the cold, crying out all the energy that had been released when I pried my body open. I had noticed on the way in that Christmas wreaths adorned many of the graves, special ones all alike, obviously mandated by the cemetery administration. Suddenly I couldn't stand to think that Phil's grave was bare. I drove to the office and bought one and brought it back.

I scratched and pounded, trying to force the metal prongs of the wreath's stand into the frozen earth, but I couldn't penetrate even a tiny bit. As I piled tiny mounds of the still meager snow around each of the three posts, it struck me: here I am, decorating for Christmas. I am not readying a warm, light-filled house for Phil's return. Instead, I am scratching the frozen earth around his grave.

We could not stay in Minneapolis. Too many memories, too many triggers would make the holiday simply unbearable for the whole family. We called our real estate agent in California, the one who had helped us find our new property, and we asked him to find us a house to rent there for the holidays. We vowed to get away from it all, the parties, the revelry, the shopping. We left the three kings, the red felt stockings, the sleigh bells, bows, and sparkling balls untouched in the basement. We regretted invitations. We kept the oven cold, ignored the Christmas music sitting on the shelf, and waited until we could escape at last.

This year would have no gift giving. I couldn't face the music in the shopping malls, the bustle, having to watch other mothers buy presents for their children. I couldn't imagine wanting anything myself, because the only thing I wanted was out of the question.

We called the Minnesota Nature Conservancy, and we learned that a stretch of land on the north shore of Lake Superior was being restored to natural wilderness, to be protected for all time against development and tourism. The Conservancy needed money for the project, a gap they still had to fill before it could happen. We filled the gap. We made a list of each person to whom we would normally have given a Christmas gift, and we made the gift instead to the Nature Conservancy in each of their names, in memory of Phil. A friend had commissioned a beautiful piece of calligraphy for us earlier in the fall of the quote from Phil's thesis we had used on his funeral program. "If we listen hard enough," it said, if we hear creation being silenced and the disappearance of natural sounds, "we can strive to make important changes while we still have the chance." We designed a card with the calligraphy on the front in a deep forest green, and we mailed one to each friend and family member instead of a Christmas present.

Jean Vail was leading a Saturday morning Advent meditation at St. Mark's. I decided to go. Because I had no shopping to do, the meditation seemed a good way to spend the time. She read the Nativity several times, and each time she asked the retreat participants to imagine ourselves as a different character or aspect of the story. Then, after each reading, we were given time for reflection to think about how her words played out in our own lives.

Experiencing the story from so many points of view was strange: to be Bethlehem itself, to be a shepherd in the fields, to become Joseph, then Mary, then one of the Magi. But the exercise was rich and creative, and I lost myself in each version of the familiar tale.

As Bethlehem, I felt strange and out of place as a bustling city, teeming with noisy activity and crowded with people bent on their agendas. I knew that this year I had become the quiet manger, tucked out of the way, an empty place where new and sacred life would be welcome, would find a fertile place to be born.

As a shepherd, I felt awed by the star-filled firmament. Ever since Phil's death, I had looked at the night sky in a new way—open to the spheres, transported and drawn to the mystery. I felt too their poverty of spirit. In grief I was bereft, humbled, ready to follow a promising star wherever it might lead.

Finally, as Mary, I found a mentor within myself, a woman who was receptive and responsive to God's invitation to bear a son, whatever his future might hold. I tried to hold on to her attitude of surrender and, knowing that one day she also would lose her son, I could see that she would accept that too and seek to discover the fruits that his death would bear.

We attended one Christmas party the night before we left. The house was lit with candles, the tree glowing with colored lights. Everyone was dressed to the nines, full of holiday cheer. The food and drink were plentiful. They had hired a small group to sing carols. Dressed in Victorian costumes, they stood on the front stairs as we gathered below them listening. I stood, holding a glass, a half grin fixed on my face. Then they launched into "White Christmas." The music pierced me, set off a wave of pain that rose, nausea in its wake. I turned in desperation, ducked into the front vestibule, and hid my face to the corner as the rest of the song buried me. But right away I felt them, friends quietly at my side, offering a freshly folded handkerchief, rubbing my back, holding me close. *This*, I thought, *is* my *gift this Christmas:* this learning, over and over, that I am loved.

The next day, we flew to California and settled into an old converted barn in the middle of the vineyards, preparing to spend our first Christmas without Phil. The house was cozy and warm, with a big stone fireplace and a wall of windows overlooking a friendly deck with a view out over the rows of vines. Our bedroom was a loft that looked out over the same view. In back, to the south, we peered out through the barren branches of a persimmon tree, its bright orange fruit hanging like ornaments, attracting the birds who gorged on their sweet pulp.

Heidi and Andrew drove up from San Francisco. The intervening weeks since they had left us in September seemed like a long time, and being together again felt good. As they put their bags in their rooms, I thought back on the eighteen Christmases we had all shared together. At first, as a newly blended family, issues needed to be worked out. I had announced the first year that I preferred short-needled Christmas trees, but I was silenced by groans. "Oh no!" they chorused, "We want long needles. They are so much more beautiful!" My family had always had large old-fashioned colored bulbs; they wanted tiny twinkling white lights. They went to church; we didn't. Those early Christmases felt lonely, disorienting, all of us wondering what had happened to a holiday that used to symbolize security and family togetherness. We hung the stockings next to each other along the fireplace, warily eyeing each other's traditional red receptacle, some so familiar, the others hanging like unwelcome interlopers at the party. At least, I thought with relief, both our families opened presents Christmas morning, not the night before.

Eventually, over the next few years, we worked out a compromised version that suited everyone, and those rituals became our own. We found trees that had needles somewhere between short and long. We settled on tiny twinkling colored lights, and we trooped down to St. Mark's together most Christmas Eves. I introduced my family's Christmas breakfast menu: poached eggs on hamburger patties, served between the stockings and opening the mound of presents under the tree.

Being a blended family had its difficulties. Phil's routine was predictable. He would stay with us for Christmas Eve and Christmas morning, then go over to Todd's just before lunch. Angus's three, though, had to struggle with competing demands and expectations—a mother and a father living in different parts of the country, both of whom wanted them for the holidays. Often, their mother took long trips in the last months of the year, especially as the children grew older. Those years were simple, but occasionally they had to fly off to Colorado or California, sometimes even on Christmas Day.

The year before this one—Phil's last Christmas—he had been home with us alone for the first time in years. He was so depressed about it he cried, wondering why no one else was there, accusing Angus and me of somehow ruining the holiday. I explained that the other three kids were adults now—thirty years old or slightly younger—and the time had come for them to want to be on their own. Chris had stayed in Boulder, Heidi and Andrew in California with friends.

Now, in an unfamiliar rented house, Heidi, Andrew, Angus, and I set about making it seem like Christmas for Chris, who would fly in from Boulder the next day. I found greens: unlike the pine boughs we were used to at home, these were subtly different, interesting sorts of evergreen. Red berries grew in profusion on a bush right outside the front door. We found candle holders around the house and filled them with red candles, and we built a roaring fire in the big stone fireplace.

We took a run up to our own new property, and from the middle of the wooded lot, we cut down a little fir tree, one we knew would have to go if and when we started to build a house. The tree was adorable, just chest high—a far cry from the ceiling-grazing sort we habitually parked in our living room at home. Angus and Andrew worked together to fashion a wooden stand, and they stretched the one cord of lights we had stashed in our suitcase straight up the tree's slim trunk. Heidi and I strung cranberries and popcorn into garlands. We rolled out spicy dough and cut out gingerbread people and stars. We took frosting tubes and gave each one a special character: a choir-boy, a Santa, a clown. We made a Phil cookie sporting a tattoo, a T-shirt, sunglasses, and a baseball hat. Chris arrived that night, and we proudly showed him the tree, sparkling in front of the window that overlooked the valley.

The rules on present-giving were clear: none allowed. Instead, we drew names out of a hat, the five of us. On Christmas Eve day, we all headed into the little town of St. Helena and—governed by a strict maximum budget—shopped for just one present for the person we had drawn. As the sun set, we lit the candles and a fire, and the kids volunteered to cook dinner. We played Christmas music and sat down to a thoroughly nontraditional Christmas Eve meal: a first course of artichokes; then lamb chops, an array of fresh grilled vegetables, pasta with homemade pesto; and raspberry sorbet and cookies for dessert. We ignored the presence of an Episcopal church a mile or so away. Instead, we sat together around the fire, listened to music, lulled by the comfort of each others' familiar voices.

On the night before Christmas, Angus and I traditionally would spend hours stuffing stockings and assembling presents under the tree. Tonight we just lay close together, not sleeping. Our bedroom loft was open and exposed, and—for the second night in a row now—we were kept half awake by an insistent murmur from Heidi's room directly below us. She had a new boyfriend. He was home near Chicago staying with his parents for Christmas, and she was talking with him on the phone. She had told us that afternoon that she was very excited about him. "I've known from the very beginning," she said, "that he is just the kind of guy I've always pictured I'd end up with." Now, as we lay there, we heard the sounds of muffled giggles, the low drone of her end of the conversation. After what seemed like hours, we finally drifted off to sleep, lulled by the sound of it, just as we had the night before.

The next morning, we had no Christmas stockings awaiting us. We jettisoned our usual breakfast menu in favor of fresh scones from the bakery shop. Then we gathered around the fire and opened, one by one with great ceremony, the single Christmas present we had been given. Each gift was carefully chosen, and no one felt deprived. We took a long hike up into the state park, along a roaring creek that rushed at the foot of towering redwoods. Then we came home, sat in the barn house's hot tub, and watched the sun set over the mountain range that frames the valley.

We had never waited until evening for Christmas dinner, but this time we did. We cooked a turkey on the grill (another first); made garlic mashed potatoes, rutabaga, asparagus, and a steamed persimmon pudding using fruit from the tree in our backyard. After dinner, we gathered around and watched videos of Phil: the one he made for Elizabeth on her birthday and the long interviews sent to us by his uncle Pock. A gaping hole was in our midst, but we were drawn together in our longing and in our grief. We looked at each other before bed and agreed: Phil would have loved this Christmas. Even without him—clearly because of him—it had been our best ever.

CHAPTER 20

Something to Leave the World

There is not one big cosmic meaning for all, there is only the meaning we each give to our life, an individual meaning, an individual plot, like an individual novel, a book for each person.

Anais Nin

Spring, the first year after Phil's death: one morning, after a meeting in our Hungry Mind Press office, my partner Gail approached me. "I really think we should talk some more about trying to publish your book," she said. I shook my head sadly. After Phil died, the book had felt obsolete to me. He appeared in so many chapters. The book was written by the mother of a living son, someone with a set of expectations to which I could no longer lay claim. I was different now, not the same person. Surely the book was no longer valid.

But Gail protested. No, she said, the book is the story of a spiritual awakening that has its own integrity, one that applies for a reader regardless of the change in your circumstances. She believed in the book, felt strongly that it should see the light of day. The rejection the manuscript had received from its first foray into the publishing world still depressed me, and I was even less optimistic about its chances now that everything had changed. She handed me a copy of *Publishers Weekly*, an issue featuring religious publishers. "Here," she said. "I have highlighted six publishers that I think would be interested. Won't you just try these?" I looked at her, wavering, afraid to say yes. The whole idea of publishing the manuscript scared me. To have written it as a journal, then as an academic thesis was one thing, but I couldn't imagine putting my personal spiritual struggle out there, letting the whole world into my inner life.

The book had begun as a journal I had kept in that year-long History of Christian Spirituality class, one I had taken as part of my Master's in Liberal Studies program three years before. I had approached the professor, asking whether he might consider letting me keep a journal on all of the ancient writers we were studying instead of choosing just one as the subject of a term paper. Recording my responses, the act of writing itself, had helped me understand the work. Relating it to my own life let me cut through the dense, difficult material and make sense of the words. He was reluctant to let me do it, to give me permission to approach the course in a different way from the rest of the class. At last he had agreed to let me start, with the condition that I show him a sample about a third of the way through the semester. One night, after reading it, he stopped me before class. He liked the journal and even suggested I turn it into a book that he would help me get published.

I was astounded. I never thought for a minute that the book part would really happen. When the semester was over, I couldn't even think about it being published, but I decided then to keep working on it, to expand it, and to grow it into my master's synthesis project the following year. He never wavered. Right up through graduation, he had insisted that I work to publish it. Now here was Gail adding her voice to his.

I considered the possibilities. My husband's roommate and his wife, who had taken the manuscript with them after that fateful weekend at our house, had been enthusiastic. Some of my friends who read it had told me it helped them wrestle with questions that plagued their own spiritual lives. Maybe the book could help people if they read about my own struggle to make sense of these difficult questions. Then—and this thought hovered—maybe, if I could no longer leave behind a child, maybe, just maybe, I could give the world a book. . . .

I looked at Gail. "OK," I said shakily. "I will agree to send the manuscript to these six publishers. But if they all turn it down, will *you* agree to let the whole thing drop?"

She shrugged. "Sure, if that's the way you want it."

I went home and wrote a cover letter, one in which I said that I knew the chapters on my son would have to be rewritten. I made six copies of the manuscript and mailed them off. I went easily to sleep that night, knowing the odds were about a thousand to one.

As the weeks, then months went by, the rejection notices were arriving in my mail. The first two came quickly, one right on the heels of the other. They were form letters, one of which didn't even bother to type in my name. "Your book doesn't fit our publishing program," they said definitively. "Good luck in finding another home for the manuscript." Then I began receiving more personal, thoughtful denials. "Your book is too heavy on the history, the portraits of the wisdom figures," one said; "there is not enough memoir." Another declared: "too much memoir, too much you, not enough historical material." Each letter hurt. Each editor stuck a finger in my gut and twisted, each time a little harder, with a little more *umph*. Not only did I vow I wouldn't touch the balance of the manuscript until I knew I had a publisher, I had long since decided I could not rewrite any of the passages about Phil. That aspect of the book was too organic, too integrated with all the other material.

Then one day, a letter arrived from a New York–based publisher. "I have read your manuscript with considerable interest," said the editor. "I will be on vacation during the next couple of weeks, but I plan to share it with some of my colleagues during that time." I stared at the piece of paper. They were *interested*? In *my* book? *No. Do not get excited. This means nothing. The same thing happened last year with the West Coast publisher.*

A few days later, I found a message in my box at Hungry Mind Press: an editor had called from another of the publishers, St. Mary's Press. He wanted to talk with me as soon as possible. I dialed the number on the slip. "Oh hi, Margaret," he said in a warm, friendly voice. "Thanks for calling back. We love your book. In fact, we'd like to go ahead with it."

"You want to 'go ahead'? What do you mean by that, *publish* it?"

"That's what I said." My heart felt a *zap* like a lightning strike.

"But what about the balance—between memoir and historical material?" I asked stupidly, suddenly incredulous that I was handing him a reason to turn it down.

"Oh, we like that just the way it is," he said. "It really works. But there is one thing I wanted to mention; it's kind of personal." I waited, expecting the worst, some request that would bring me back down to earth, make the whole thing impossible. "You mentioned in your letter that you knew you would have to rewrite the chapters that involve your son." He paused, offered some kind, gentle words of condolence about Phil's death. Then he went on. "We don't think you can do that. We think it's better to leave the book as it stands and have you write a new prologue about your loss."

I stood there, holding the phone, barely breathing. They were serious. They really wanted to publish it! He went on to discuss details of scheduling, the editing process, a contract. . . . I was barely listening, paying attention only to the leaping in my gut, the dance my feet wanted to do. At last I hung up. I looked at Tia sitting at my feet. "*Did you hear that?*" I shouted. "They want to publish my book!"

That night I had a dream in which I was riding on a tall sailing ship wearing the black flowing robe I had taken home from my graduate-school commencement ceremony. In the dream, the robe was much too big, flapping in the wind, hampering my efforts to steer. I had stolen the ship and was trying to sail it, but I couldn't get the hang of how it worked. Where did the wind come from? If I tried to go left, the ship went right; if I turned right, we spun around. I was at the helm, but utterly illegitimate. I was afraid, afraid I would be "found out," the ship taken away from me, but yet I wanted to sail, to let the wind take hold and fly me out to sea.

When I woke up, I knew that the dream was about my writing life, about how awkward I felt acknowledging that this new activity I had grown to love was real. I could never seem to claim out loud that I was "a writer."

A couple of days later, a friend handed me a slip of paper on which was written a quote from Nelson Mandela's inaugural speech in 1994: "Our deepest fear is not that we are inadequate. Our deepest fear is that we are powerful beyond measure."

CHAPTER 21

Nancy

Tell me about despair, yours, and I will tell you mine.
Meanwhile the world goes on. . . .

Mary Oliver

Nancy had been struggling with her cancer ever since she found out about it, just the week before Phil's accident. Early on, when it was discovered in her lungs, they had trouble even determining its source, its primary site. Eventually they decided it was ovarian cancer, a difficult type that was elusive to treatment. But Nancy had approached this disease as she did so much of her life. She felt strongly that the cancer was a sign, a message to her from her body that something was spiritually amiss. She set about listening, opening her heart, and concentrating far more on her soul—on examining and healing her mental blocks and channels—than she did on worrying about the fate of her body. The body, she believed, would take care of itself once the spiritual path was clear.

She still sought treatment. She had consulted specialists, received multiple opinions, bravely withstood one long round of chemotherapy, and would have to endure another before too long. Her hair had fallen out, and she was sporting a wig with panache.

Meanwhile, I was in denial. I needed her too much even to entertain the possibility that she might die. I was so self-absorbed, coping with my own grief, that I had little room for anyone else's problems, even one this huge.

Late in the fall, a friend had called to tell me that an organization she was involved in was designing a citywide conference for the spring. To give a focus to the event, they were planning to present an award to a Woman of Distinction. We both agreed that Nancy would be a perfect nominee. If she won, it would come at a time when she needed a boost, and no one could be more deserving of recognition. I obtained a copy of the application guidelines and sat down to write about my friend and why she should receive the award.

I wrote that she was not a breaker of glass ceilings, sitting victorious on top of some corporate pyramid, but that she was powerful nonetheless, wielding the power of humility, service, self-sacrifice, and surrender. I wrote about her years as a social worker in Bedford-Stuyvesant, her two years in Bógota, Colombia, and her years with our own county welfare department working with child abuse before it became a high-profile problem. I wrote about her work with Smith College, designing programs to mentor young women, and of her decision to seek a master's degree at a local seminary in her forties and to take up a new career in spiritual direction. Finally, I wrote about her cancer and her characteristically insightful and dignified experience with her disease.

In March 1996, eight months after Phil died, Nancy and I flew to Tucson, Arizona, for a few days' escape at Canyon Ranch, a center for health and fitness in the desert foothills of the Catalina Mountains. I had been there before, and I had suggested the trip to Nancy around Christmastime. I knew she would find support there for her holistic approach to healing cancer. Mostly, though, the move was selfish on my part. I wanted us to go away alone for a few days together. With

Phil's death and her disease, I had felt remote from my old friend, as if these life-changing events had robbed us of our relationship, and I wanted it back.

The weather was sunny and warmer at Canyon Ranch than March was back home in Minnesota, but our energy levels were far apart. Nancy moved tentatively, carefully. She wore a turban on her head by then, and a slow walk around the grounds was all the exercise she could manage. While I spent my mornings and afternoons working out in the gym, hiking in the desert, or biking, she had signed up for biofeedback lessons, meditation sessions, and a workshop on stress reduction techniques.

We took all our meals together, and now at lunch on our last day, I leaned across the table, studying her face, searching her eyes. I kept looking for the old spark, waiting for us to start giggling at something happening at a nearby table as we used to do, but a new soberness had settled over the two of us like an oppressive heat wave. I couldn't find the way back to the old Nancy I used to know. I couldn't seem to tap into a vein of lightness or sunshine. After lunch, we posed for a picture together, standing in front of a bed of colorful pansies, arms linked around each others' shoulders, smiling for the camera. The photo was another in a long tradition of such shots, and I realized that it might be our last.

Nancy won the Woman of Distinction award. On a blustery day toward the end of April, I stood at the podium in a convention hall filled with women. She was unable to be there, lying at the Mayo Clinic, her lungs full of fluid, her breath short, her energy spent. I was proud of my friend, proud to read the words that I had written about her, proud to bear witness to our friendship and to the fineness of this woman whom I knew and loved. I spoke slowly, knowing they were videotaping the presentation for her, and I tried hard not to cry.

The next night, Angus and I were unpacking in our San Francisco hotel room, preparing to go out to dinner with Heidi and her new boyfriend Caley, the one who had spent hours on the other end of the phone over Christmas. We were going to meet him at last, this voice who increasingly answered the phone at her apartment when we called.

I had flown out to California in a daze that afternoon, weighed down by the growing realization that I was losing my best friend. Nancy had been scheduled for major surgery that day. Just as we were leaving for the restaurant, the phone in our hotel room rang. Nancy's husband gave me the bad news: the cancer had spread extensively throughout her abdominal area. They had removed everything they could find, but she was in terrible pain. I was halfway across the country. I couldn't go to her, couldn't do anything to help. I was too numb from the news even to remember my own grief. I was thinking only of Nancy, of her husband, of her daughter and son.

Where was God in this?

Nancy had, in the last few years, developed a spiritual perspective that did not always resonate with mine. If, for example, she was driving a car full of mentally handicapped people from the drop-in center she volunteered for and a parking place suddenly opened up, she would later tell me about it joyously, convinced that God was rewarding her for her efforts. The corollary of that perspective, in my mind, was that her cancer was a deliberate consequence of some reprehensible deed, a merciless punishment that she deserved. I could not subscribe to that theory any more than I could accept that Phil's death was a deliberate Godly swipe at me.

No. God was unable to stop the spread of Nancy's cancer, unable to keep Phil and Sean from slipping on the ice. I needed to look for God instead in grace: in the forces of the universe that flowed toward the positive. I could find grace in our trip to Canyon Ranch together, in Nancy's winning the Woman of Distinction award.

Just before leaving for the airport that morning, my business partner Page had approached me tentatively. "I am worried," she said,

"that you will somehow think we are suggesting Phil can be replaced."
I waited, not knowing what was coming. "But Maxwell is being chris-
tened in May, and Jay and I would like it very much if you would be
his godmother." I was surprised, flattered, and excited. Of course!
What could be better now than to have this two-year-old for a special
friend?

We sat, Angus, Heidi, and I, crowded into a booth in a hip, noisy San
Francisco restaurant. Around us, a trendy young crowd filled the air
with a deafening din of cocktail and dinner chatter. We were waiting
for Caley. I looked up. Heading toward us was a friendly looking,
Angus-sized young man. He wore fashionable round glasses and a big
smile, a shock of straight dark bangs falling over one eyebrow. His
brown eyes were direct and strong, and his manner assured. He was a
medical student at the University of California San Francisco, three
years younger than Heidi. Angus and I had been increasingly eager to
meet him, wondering how he would be, whether he would seem too
young for her, whether we would like this young man who loomed
large in her future.

We spent a delicious couple of hours over dinner. Caley was
adorable. His smile was genuine, joy-filled, open. He is an only child,
and he obviously knew he was loved. He was bright, ambitious, and
full of energy. He was funny, warm, and quick. He adored Heidi; that
much was clear. Despite his lag of three years, he clearly carried
weight in the relationship. The dynamics felt good. When we
returned to our room, we looked at each other. I could tell right away
that Angus had liked him too. "He's a good guy," he pronounced.
Knowing Angus as I do, that was all he needed to say, and it was high
praise.

I lay in bed that night, feeling suspended, as if I were weightless,
floating alone in space. Here I was, in the middle of my life. On the
one hand, everything was falling apart. My only son was dead, my best

friend was dying. I was scared, angry, and confused. I was disoriented, not used to life presenting itself in this form. On the other hand, I had received the promise of new life: being Maxwell's godmother, the possibility that Heidi and Caley might marry some day and give us a grandchild, albeit not of my own genes. As I lay there, I became aware that deep, deep inside of me was an untouchable core, a precious inner sanctum that was insulated from all these things happening around me, both the bad and the good. That center seemed to burn like a pilot light, a constant, dependable source of energy whose flame held steady no matter what happened on the outside. Was that ineffable center in the depths of my being a connection to everything else, my link to a unity in which I participated? Could I learn to tune in to that place more regularly, to rely on its steady flame in the face of the unpredictable swirl of life around me?

It was May, time for warmth and sunshine, the advent of summer. But on an unseasonably cold day—exactly nine months after Phil's death—I was inside, still crying. I called my mother, then Nancy, anyone who would listen, anyone who still had the patience to let me talk, to put up with the endless stream of grief and pain.

Nancy told me that I was doing exactly what I was supposed to do. "You are being led," she said. "There are so many tears inside you, and they just have to come out." As I threw the wadded pieces of Kleenex one after another into the wastebasket, I was reminded of Nancy's wound.

About a week after she had returned from the hospital from her last surgery, I was sitting at her bedside helping her change the dressing on her surgical incision. Infection had set in, and in the center of the line of stitches was a hole, a deep, black hole, out of which relentlessly flowed dark yellow pus that filled gauze pad after gauze pad. The flow stopped briefly, but Nancy had to work to keep it open, to keep the pus coming. "The doctor says we can't let it knit over on the surface," she said. "It has to be kept open so it can heal, beginning at the very bottom, slowly filling layer by layer until it is completely healed from the bottom up. Only then can the skin be allowed to close over."

As I helped her, carefully wiping the wound's surface, I knew that my grieving heart was like her weeping sore. Keeping the wound open was important: to let it disrupt life now and then, to miss meetings when I had to, to let work suffer and put my energy toward healing those inner layers beneath the surface. I had to give myself permission to stop running around, to stop meeting every deadline and returning every phone call; instead I needed to keep the channels open, to stay home for a day and let the tears flow.

As the month of May rolled into June, life was a constant struggle: to do what I had to do for Hungry Mind Press and its never-ending publication deadlines and at the same time to stay present for Nancy in her continuing decline. I would drive to our office, pick up cover designs or copy, meet with my partners, then drive to Nancy's house to take my turn with her other friends waiting to see her, one by one. Sometimes she was attentive, wanting to do projects, have her mail read to her, write notes; other times she had little energy and only wanted to be read to. She was consistently optimistic, convinced that she would triumph over the disease. "I think this is only the dark night of the soul," she said. "I know I'm going to get better and beat this thing." Then, proud of the new gray crew cut that was growing back on her head, she'd say, "I've decided I'm going to become one of those chic older women who wear big earrings and have their silver hair cut close to their heads."

A couple of times I wanted to pour out my feelings to her, tell her how much I loved her, how much she had meant to me, how I would never forget her. But I was silent instead, afraid to burst her bubble, afraid my own pessimism was out of line.

One day she took my hand and looked directly into my eyes, her own face hollow and mysterious. "I'm afraid this isn't going to work out. I don't think I'm going to get better," she said slowly. I tightened my grip on her cold, thin fingers. Looking at her, I felt that I was looking through her to a different realm, one that was forbidden to me but one to which my own son was privy.

"I'm going to die too, you know," I said. "It's just that you know how and more closely when." I waited a few breaths, thought about how she was about to embark on a great adventure. "It's exciting, really," I said, almost as if she were leaving on an exotic trip abroad. "Just think: you get to find out what happens when we die. The mysteries we have wondered about so long will be finally clear to you." I meant it. In an odd way I actually felt I envied her for a minute, but then a lump appeared in the back of my throat, and I just sat there holding her hand while she closed her eyes.

In late June, we received a worried phone call from Andrew. He was in Colorado where he and Chris had been backpacking together in the mountains. That morning, as they were checking out of a bed and breakfast they had stayed in at the end of the trip, Chris had been overcome by a horrible stomachache—so painful that he could only roll on the floor, moaning. Andrew had driven him to a hospital nearby, and there they had spent the day, Chris on morphine, the doctors debating what to do. Late that night, he woke us with another call. They had finally done emergency surgery and found that Chris's appendix had ruptured hours before; there was a serious, extensive peritonitis infection. Their mother, who lived nearby, came immediately to be with them. We packed our things and headed for Glenwood Springs, Colorado.

Chris lay on the pillows, flushed, listless, his usual upbeat energy dissipated. He couldn't muster the strength even to sit up, to hold a newspaper. Normally ravenous, he could eat nothing. There were intravenous tubes hanging from stands pumping painkillers and antibiotics into his system. I felt a rush of love, of tender care, suddenly aware of how much this almost-son meant to me, of the place he held in my heart—not like a friend, like precious family. Doctors stopped by regularly, anxiously watching for change. A new, rare, and unusual bacteria had grown from the infection, and they couldn't seem to find the right antibiotic to fight it. Angus and I could hardly believe what was happening. Yet another of our children threatened in this way, so soon. At last, having consulted other sources, the doctors came up with a new medication to try. Chris swallowed a couple of pills, and we left for the night, still worried.

When we arrived at the hospital the next morning, Chris was sitting up in bed smiling. Overnight, he had changed dramatically. His color was good, his energy back. We breathed a huge sigh of relief. Later that afternoon—when, to our surprise, they pronounced him ready to leave—we packed his things and drove him back to his house in Boulder. We settled in to his spare room for the next couple of days, went to the grocery store for him, did the laundry, and made sure he could cope. Monday around noon, we had our bags packed, ready to leave for Minneapolis.

The phone rang. Chris couldn't move very fast, so I ran to answer it for him. My own mother was on the line. "Oh . . ." she said. "I was kind of hoping Angus would answer." Her voice was heavy, sodden.

"What is it?" I said, my heart beating faster and faster as I slowly grasped her tone.

"It's Nancy, sweetie. She's dead."

We drove to the Denver airport and boarded the plane in a blur. In Minneapolis we drove straight to Nancy's house. I was met at the door by one of our friends, teary-eyed and tired. "She's still here if you want to see her," she said. "We've been fighting off the coroner."

Still here . . . her body? I couldn't believe it. I knew I had to see her. I climbed the stairs, approached her bedroom door, which was closed as it had been so many times in my recent visits. I put my hand on the knob, turned it tentatively, and pushed the door slowly open, brushing the carpeted floor.

The room is clean, spotlessly arranged. Vases of flowers are everywhere. The light is dim; candles flicker from tabletops. I find another friend sitting by the bedside, but on seeing me she stands up to leave. I take her place, settling in slowly on the familiar white wicker chair. Nancy is lying there peacefully, wearing her pink and blue satin robe, her head on neatly plumped pillows, her hands folded on top of the smooth, perfectly made bed. I have never seen a dead body like this before, never so close, never of someone I love this much. I stare. I warily put my hands on top of hers. They are cold. Her face is totally peaceful, not a wrinkle anywhere, as if she has become suddenly young. Her eyes are closed, her lips drawn back into a half smile. I can see that this is a body, not a person. "She" is gone, but here she is. I kiss her cold forehead; I smooth her still-soft crop of short hair.

I tell her all those things that I had wanted to say in our last days together: how much fun we have had, how much wisdom she has given to me, how much I love her, how much I will miss her. As I talk, I feel as if she is still near, as if she can hear what I am saying. I am aware that none of this is news to her, that she knows, has always known.

Here she was, and here was I. Phil was dead, but my life stretched out ahead of me forty, maybe fifty years. I had people to love and things to do. I was not ready to trade places with Nancy.

As I sat and looked at her vacant body, as I absorbed death in all its finality, I wondered how the scene would have been if I had gone to be with Phil's body, if I had flown out to Seattle after all, if I had entered the cold chambers of the medical examiner's office and sat next to the table on which he lay. I understood that sitting with Nancy's body, seeing it and touching it would be an important piece in my grieving process for her. I felt oddly complete, as if I could now let go of her physical self and move on to the process of living with her in spirit.

As I tiptoed out of the room, I noticed, along with the sadness for Nancy, a nagging regret—a kind of shame, really—that I had not been able to honor my own son with the same kind of visit.

CHAPTER 22

The Body's Code

Written on the body is a secret code only
visible in certain lights, the accumulations
of a lifetime gather there.

Jeanette Winterson

In the many books I had read on grief in the weeks and months since
Phil's death, I had noticed near unanimity on the importance of seeing the loved one's body, particularly after the death of a child. They
agreed that it made a huge difference to see the physical remains, to
touch death, to come to terms with the reality of this new absence.
When we had dinner in New York with the Ryans, Judy had told us
about how they had spent time with Sean's body, how she remembered stroking the soft hair on his arm. They had been in shock, felt
very anxious, almost panicky, but they were still glad they had opted
to bring Sean home, to see his body as a way of saying good-bye. After
my visit with Nancy, I became increasingly uneasy with how we had
chosen, in the confusing hours of shock after Phil's death, to deal with
his body.

One day, I was talking with a friend whose stepson had been
thrown from a car in Arizona and killed. She mentioned that pictures
from his autopsy had clarified one of the questions they had about the

accident. *Pictures?* My heart froze around this word. I knew they had done an autopsy on Phil, but I had never thought about pictures. What if there were some? Maybe I could see them. If it was too late to spend time with his body, would seeing pictures somehow bring me the closure I felt I was lacking? The thought of seeing photos was terrifying, but I knew I had to find out if this was a possibility.

I dialed a number I had found on Phil's death certificate, the number of the Tacoma medical examiner's office. An answering machine gave me several options, out of which I chose a woman's name, a place to begin. Her voice was friendly, kind. I told her who I was and what I wanted. She put me on hold.

After what seemed a very long time, a doctor came on the phone. I asked him about the photos. He said they existed but that I probably would not like to see them.

"His face was basically crushed. I wouldn't want to send you these pictures, because that's the last way you would remember him." He told me that if I sent in fifteen dollars, they would send me a copy of the report, preferably without pictures.

I hung up the phone, shaking. I couldn't banish an image of Phil, his face distorted, lying on a table, the life gone out of him. But I was glad I had made the call. I felt sad but reassured about our original decision not to go to Washington. I really might have had a hard time remembering him any other way. At least what I pictured now was only in my imagination.

Several days later, the autopsy report arrived: pages and pages of description of Phil, every detail of the broken body I had never seen. My hands shook. My stomach churned. I sat down in an armchair and read every word slowly, hungrily, carefully. As I read, I found not body parts but memories, not clinical observations but stories that flooded my head and heart.

Scalp hair is reddish, short and straight . . .

Actually, his hair was black when he was born, odd, dark fine plumage, but it all fell out at a couple of weeks and grew back in, pure white. At six months or so, it stood up all over his head—a radiant aura that made him look as if he had stuck his finger in a socket. Then, as he grew, it leveled out straight, and he wore it in a bowl cut, like a white helmet shining in the sun. One summer, when I was working full-time, I signed Phil up for an urban program called "Summer in the City." He and twenty or so other inner-city residents were taken on a bus every day for a week or two to see all the points of cultural interest. Late one afternoon, I was there to meet the bus when he stepped off at the end of the day. He and a little girl hopped off, the only other white child in the program. After we drove away, he turned to me. "They call Courtney 'Cornball,'" he said sadly.

"That's too bad," I said. "I'll bet that hurts her feelings."

He nodded. His lip began to tremble, tears forming at the inside edges of his eyes. "And they call me 'Snowball'."

Bruises, cuts, abrasions, a deep laceration of the lower lip . . .

But what about the scar? Why didn't they mention the scar, a straight-line dent in the skin that angled downward from the left eyebrow? Seven years before, bored, chin in my hand, I looked out in a daze over the soccer field as I had on so many fall afternoons. A small group of uniformed players knotted on the right defense side of the field. "It's Phil!" someone shouted, and my heart stopped. There he was, lying on the grass, surrounded by worried teammates. I ran to the sidelines, held back from the field by the unspoken rule that mothers were not welcome at a time like this. The cut was big—a slice really— dangerously close to his eye. The emergency room doctor was nice, and I remember being almost ecstatic at this injury: so harmless, so unthreatening, just texture to give his face a little character.

There is abrasion and bruising of the right ear. . . .

But what about the left one? They must have missed the tiny dot, the hole in his earlobe. At twelve, he came to me one summer day. His friend Andrew showed up wearing a safety pin through his ear. Phil wanted to do it too. I thought a minute. "Oh, excellent!" I said, looking as excited as I could. "I have so many pairs of earrings where one is lost. You could put those singles to good use." The risk was a calculated one, and that day it worked. Five years later, though, just before high school graduation, he showed up with a stud in his left ear. By then it was commonplace, a manageable, tame sort of rebellion. By sophomore year in college, the earring was gone. Last time I looked, I couldn't even see the hole. It was nothing a medical examiner would notice.

The upper and lower jaws contain natural teeth. . . .

But they didn't notice the artificial cap, upper right front tooth. A call from school, sixth-grade gym. Dodgeball. He was in the middle of the circle, and a classmate made a big-armed direct hit. On the mouth. The tooth chipped off. The temporary turned gray. This permanent cap did look real, no doubt about it.

Other pelvic organs and external genital organs are examined and reveal no evidence of trauma. . . .

In the hospital, just after Phil was born, our pediatrician stopped by one morning on his rounds. He wanted to know whether we wanted to have Phil circumcised. "We don't really have any medical reasons to recommend it these days," he said.

"Are *you* circumcised?" I asked the doctor, surprised that he was so unenthusiastic about a procedure I had always assumed would take place just after birth.

"As a matter of fact, I'm not," he replied, slightly embarrassed by my directness. Todd and I debated. Should Phil be made to look like his dad? What about school friends and inevitable comparisons in the locker room. Maybe, surely, it would hurt. The next morning, we opted to do nothing, to spare Phil a painful operation in his first week of life.

There are tattoos noted on the body. The left leg in the region of the ankle shows a tattoo depicting what appears to be a sunrise. . . .

It was a warm April day, spring vacation, 1992. We were walking side by side several blocks to a neighborhood pizza grill for lunch, just the two of us. I looked down at his ankle, just above the strap of his sandals. "What's that?" I asked. "Did you do it with a ballpoint pen?" It was a simple jagged drawing of a mountain with a half sun and rays rising above it. "No, Mom, it's a tattoo," he said. "I've had it since Thanksgiving," he said. "It's just been under my sock until now."

There is also a tattoo in the right deltoid region depicting a man and a woman. . . .

But it was not a man and a woman, rather a Buddha and a goddess on a lotus. He had it done several years later, at Bates. The image came from a book I had given him, *The Gaia Principle.* He told me right away this time, on the phone. "Did it hurt?" I asked.

"Like hell," he groaned.

I flipped over the last page of the report and leaned back, closed my eyes. At last I had done it: spent time with his body. Some aspects of the report surprised me: mild arterial sclerosis, for example. Had all that fast food already taken its toll? Would he have died of a heart attack, leaving a young family? His neck had been broken, lower cervical vertebrae. I thought about what it could have meant if he had lived with an injury like that. For a moment I was almost relieved that he died, that he was not lying somewhere in a hospital, paralyzed from the neck down.

I now knew how much his heart weighed, his kidney, his liver, and his brain. I knew the length and breadth of the cuts and bruises that killed him. But the tattoos finally did it; the tattoos wiped out any remaining doubt. Whatever small voice deep in my consciousness still held out hope that they had the wrong guy—that his ring had been found on someone else—had been silenced forever. The autopsy report was not the same as seeing his dead body, but at least I felt I had done all that I could do.

CHAPTER 23

Return to the Mountain

We need to sit on the rim
of the well of darkness
and fish for fallen light
with patience.

Pablo Neruda

Nicole and I had been burning up the telephone wires ever since she left Minneapolis after Phil's funeral. She had moved back to Seattle where she and Phil had lived together, in the shadow of Mount Rainier. She worked in a restaurant to pay the rent, but she had also landed herself an internship at a small Seattle-based book publishing company. I never worried that I would bore her with a dream about Phil or that I would drag her down with my pain. She always understood exactly how I felt. She could never shock me nor I her with our neediness or the depth of our despair.

In February, I put together my frequent flyer miles and sent Nicole a ticket to Minneapolis. Six months had passed since Phil's death, and we both longed to be together. Tia's excitement was heartrending. She smelled Nicole, whined, leaped for joy. But where was Phil? She ran behind her, checked the empty car from which she had just emerged. I hugged my new young friend, gazing long and hard at her bright face, her fiery eyes. Her high-pitched voice, so full of energy, humor, and appreciation, was music to my ears. I installed her across the hall from Phil's room, and each morning Tia would push the door open, rooting in the sheets with her nose, impatient to wake her Frisbee-playing companion.

We visited the contemporary art museum and sat long over lunch in the cafeteria. We talked about books and publishing, how Nicole might learn the skills she needed to go into the business. She came with me to a meeting of the Hungry Mind Press partners, listened to us plan the books for the next season, helped brainstorm a title change, compared several sketches of a cover design.

Back home we sat together over her album of pictures of Phil. The book contained so many I had never seen before, pose after pose of his easy, comfortable way, his smiling face, his devil-may-care attitude, his openness, his friendly, warm face. He would have been a wonderful partner for her, I thought, and she the daughter-in-law I had always dreamed of. In her presence, I felt expanded, as if being with the woman Phil loved brought me into his life again, into the orbit of his being, alive or dead. But I knew, as we sat there, that I had no claim on her.

"Nicole, you know Phil would want you to love again, to go on with your life." I meant it, and I knew that at some level she needed to have my permission, to know that I expected and wanted her to find another man.

On the third day, we were loading the car with her bags, ready to head for the airport. She held out the bouquet of tulips I had placed by her bed, now sagging, the stems limply hanging their heads. "You can put these in Phil's room," she said, as she handed the vase to me, her eyes filling with tears. Then she was crying, sobbing, her breath catching and jagged. We both cried all the way to the airport.

The next morning felt like one of the first mornings. My head ached; my eyes stung. I couldn't get up, couldn't bear to face the day. I remembered then the words of a friend, one whose own son had been killed in a bicycle accident nine years before. "There will be days," she had said a few months before, leaning over the table toward me over a cup of tea, "days when it will be so bad you will think you are back to the beginning, to square one. But you won't be. Trust me, you won't be."

The day after Nicole left felt like that, but it wasn't. To my surprise, I did get up. Not only that, but I discovered later that morning a new store of energy. I found myself rooting through the boxes of photographs of Phil, extras we had found that had never been put in family albums, photos friends had sent us since his death, the store of pictures taken by his friend at Bates, the one who had done the portrait of him for her class. I spent the day doing what I had dreaded and avoided for months: cutting, arranging, and pasting the photos into a special album, a Phil album of my own. The task took hours. The work was slow, painstaking, but as I saw the collection taking shape in the book's pages, I knew the album was going to be a treasure. I even threw a few bad pictures away.

As I worked, I thought about grief and its paradox. I thought again of the article I had read the October before, the one by the West Coast professor who lost much of his family in one car accident. The title of his article was "Long Night's Journey into Light." He wrote that, just after the tragedy, he was tempted to chase desperately after the little light that remained to him. Reluctant to lose the last vestiges of day, he was grasping, running after the setting sun to grab what was left of the receding glow. Then someone told him the quickest way to the sun was to turn around and head directly into the darkness, there to meet the sunrise on the other side.

This phase of grief was like a spiral: a slow ascent, then an encounter that would send me through a loop of agony, then the beginning once again of progress. The worst pain, the most agonizing passages, seemed to work like a summer thunderstorm: they cleared the atmosphere, chased the clouds away and brought fresh, clear air, soft breezes and even sunshine in their wake. I could see how I wanted to resist and avoid those tough encounters because of the pain that would inevitably follow, but I could also see that those agonizing confrontations led to progress. "Pain," Nancy had told me once, "is the fuel we burn for the journey."

Toward the end of July, nearing the end of the first year, Nicole's twenty-fourth birthday was approaching. She called one day and announced that in honor of her birthday she was planning to climb Mount Rainier. Living in Seattle, the mountain was ever present to her, an icon looming on the horizon. Day after day she stared at it, thought about it, thought about Phil and about how she owed it to him to summit the mountain. Besides, the last time she had seen Phil was on her birthday the year before.

I was incredulous. I couldn't in my wildest dreams imagine even considering such a thing, but I also knew we were different. Like Phil, Nicole had a far greater tolerance for physical risk than I did. She was hardy, strong, young. She said that Mike Gauthier, Phil's old roommate and the chief climbing ranger, was going to lead her up on a special trip. I had no doubt that she would be in good hands and that she was up to it physically.

I also thought about the psychic aspects of the climb. I had been learning from my own experience with grief that the toughest, most confrontational things loomed largest. They seemed huge barriers on the path to recovery, but I also knew that only in going right through the middle of those impossible things could real progress be made. For Nicole to make that climb, actually to visit the spot from which Phil fell, to make it to the summit herself, could be a huge breakthrough in her ability to move forward. Still, I was terrified. "Don't tell your parents you're going to climb," I begged. "Just call them—and me—as soon as you're down safely."

The day of the climb, visiting my sister-in-law at her ranch in Wyoming, I waited for the call, but none came. At last, knowing it was well past the time she should have been back, I dialed her apartment in Seattle. She answered.

"Happy birthday," I breathed, fueling the wish with a sigh of relief at the sound of her voice.

"Thank God you called," she said. "I lost the number of the ranch, and I was afraid you would worry."

Mike Gauthier had planned a memorial service for the anniversary of Phil and Sean's deaths to be held on Mount Rainier. When he called, we accepted immediately, grateful to be able to get away from home, to have something to do to mark the occasion. Heidi and Andrew agreed to join us, my parents too, but Chris opted to stay in Boulder, to experience the anniversary on his own. I worried about that and wanted him there, but he was still recovering from his surgery a couple of months before and he did not feel up to the trip.

We set our alarms in the Seattle hotel for 4:30 A.M. and climbed in the car to make the long drive to the mountain, much as we had the September before when we took Phil's ashes to Glacier Basin. This time, though, as the sun rose, we could see that the day would be glorious. As we drove, the mountain appeared like a ghost before us, the rising sun spreading a hot blush over the surface of the snow. Road construction slowed us down, made us late, but as we drove up the winding road to the Sunrise Visitor Center, the slopes were glowing with color: blue lupine, yellow asters, Queen Anne's lace. We hiked down a path to a semicircular stone terrace that looked out over a spectacular view.

As the five of us and my parents carefully made our way down, we could see a crowd gathered there: Nicole and Jeff Cha, Bill and Judy Ryan, their two daughters and their husbands, other friends of Phil's from the Seattle area, a couple of whom had worked with him at the pizza place during his semester there a couple of years before, a knot of park rangers in uniform. A bagpipe was playing "Amazing Grace." The musician, a friend of Sean and Phil's who had wanted to play for the service the year before but had not been able to, had now come to be there with us on the anniversary. As the piercing, baleful tones threaded their way through the somber crowd, I glanced at my father. He was hunched over, his head bowed, his hands at his face. Tears were spilling down his cheeks, his shoulders were shuddering with sobs. I stared, turned inside out. It was the first time I had seen him cry since Phil's death, in fact the first time I had ever seen him—in all my fifty years—cry with open abandon.

The little ceremony was spontaneous, heartfelt. One by one, family members and friends came forward to speak. Some told stories and reminisced. Todd, who had decided not to come, had sent a letter that was read aloud. Others read passages chosen for the occasion. We had brought Phil's journal with us, marked with passages to read that he had carefully saved. Heidi and Andrew, overcome with shyness and emotion, decided at the last minute not to read, but Angus spoke, and so did Jeff Cha. Nicole had never intended to speak, feeling that her ordeal at Bates College was enough. I agreed. I didn't want to either. I was afraid I would break down, that I would embarrass myself and my family. But this service was the third I had been to, and I had never spoken for my son. I wanted to do my part, to make him proud. I stepped forward and let his own words speak for him, a poem he had written on a NOLS solo, one called "To Be a Mountain."

Sean's sister read one of Sean's favorite poems, "The Peace of Wild Things" by Wendell Berry, that Phil too had copied into his own journal.

> When despair for the world grows in me
> and I wake in the night at the least sound
> in fear of what my life and my children's lives may be,
> I go and lie down where the wood drake

rests in her beauty on the water, and the great heron feeds.
I come into the peace of wild things
who do not tax their lives with forethought
of grief. I come into the presence of still water.
And I feel above me the day-blind stars
waiting with their light. For a time
I rest in the grace of the world, and am free.

As we stood there, gathered in the morning chill, a bird appeared. It perched first, tentatively, on a branch of evergreen, directly behind and above Mike, silhouetted by the breathtaking view. Then it jumped down and landed in the middle of the circle of friends. The bird hopped along several times, pecking for crumbs, totally unafraid. Only one? No sooner had I framed the thought than another, a companion, landed gently on the evergreen branch beside us, just overhead. They are here, I thought, both of them. Their spirits live, merged with the beauty of these snow-capped peaks, this crystalline sky, these rampant wildflowers. The bagpipes whined again, and we turned and walked away.

Mike had arranged a reception with cider and food, and we all gathered, talking, showing each other pictures of Phil and Sean. The Ryans had brought camping gear and had spent the night before camping at Sunrise. That night they were planning to spend another night on the mountain. Our own little band hiked up to Glacier Basin. It was sunny and warm now, the wildflowers thick and colorful, so different from the hike we had made the year before. We could feel the beauty of the mountain and understood why Phil and Sean had been drawn to it so.

On the way down the trail, hiking beside Nicole, I said to her, "I want always to be your friend, even after you meet someone new."

She told me it was much too soon to be thinking that way, but I knew she would soon need to move on, to begin to put Phil behind her.

CHAPTER 24

Pilgrimage

We shall not cease from exploration
And the end of all our exploring
Will be to arrive where we started
And know the place for the first time.

T. S. Eliot

The first year was over. As we flew out of Seattle, looking down at the
glacier below us, Angus and I agreed we had had enough of Mount
Rainier. We had made our peace with it in a small way. I had begun to
understand Phil's love of its crisp thin air, its vistas of lupine, its majes-
tic peak looming on the horizon, but I found no comfort in its presence. Like Nicole, who was packing her things to return to
Massachusetts, I wanted mostly to turn my back on its relentless
power and leave. I knew that the possibility of total forgiveness was
remote. Better to leave the connection at this: a tenuous détente. I had
my own mountain to climb right now: a slow, steady ascent back to
life.

I understood that the spiral of grief I had experienced in the last
months would continue—perhaps for years, perhaps forever. I also
knew that I would need to undertake some deliberate strategies to
dissipate the sorrow and pain, to turn that energy in new, positive

directions. We were ready to do some traveling; my book would need to be edited for publication. We needed to go on with our lives, to turn our love and attention to the people who surrounded us, to embrace the living once again.

One day in the next couple of weeks, I was rummaging through a small wooden slotted file box in my bedroom when my fingers closed around an old letter. I noticed that it was in Phil's handwriting, and my heart leaped. I opened the neatly folded sheet of lined notebook paper and saw that it was a letter he had slipped under my door the night before he and Dryw left on their cross-country bicycle trip in the last quarter of their senior year in high school. I had forgotten all about it. "Dear Mom," it read:

> I just want to tell you in so many words—Thank you! For giving me the opportunity to go on a trip like this. Not many moms I know would have the courage to let their sons partake in such an adventure. I also want to thank you for letting me be the person I am. I'm not quite sure how to say it, but you have taught me to do the things I really love, and that it's OK to be different—and I've found out it can be very special.
>
> I know you're a bit hesitant in actually waving goodbye tomorrow—but you don't have to worry. Dryw and I will take good care of each other. I have the opportunity to learn so much in the next seven weeks, and I plan to take full advantage of it. I'll miss you and I love you! Phil.
>
> P. S. If you ever wake up and are sick with fear or worry—just look out the window at the stars and you will know that those are the exact beautiful stars I'm probably looking up at at the same moment.

Angus and I signed up for a trip to the Holy Land, to Israel. Led by David Keller, the trip was designed as a pilgrimage, not simply a historical or political quest to see the sights. When we set out, I was not so sure what I was looking for, but—as in any journey of the kind—the answers came, unbidden, as I lived the questions. We stayed in three different places—a monastery, a kibbutz, and an Arab hotel—and instead of rushing from one site to another, we took our time just sitting, absorbing the sacredness of the place, and listening to David's thoughtful, insightful reflections.

One morning we took the bus to Nazareth, the home of Jesus and his mother Mary. We visited an Orthodox church, built over a well fed by a spring in the town, presumably the one that must have been used by Mary. The apocryphal Gospel according to St. James reports that Mary was at that well when the angel of God came to her in the annunciation.

We scooped some of the water, then drank it. Then David had us stand in a circle, our empty hands cupped. In order to receive the word of God, he said, Mary had to be empty. She had to empty herself, to be utterly open, to hear. Then she was able to say, "Let it be, according to your will."

As David said those words, I felt as if he were talking to me. Just as she had been in the Advent meditation I attended, here was Mary again—in her attitude of acceptance, of transparency, a mentor for me. After all the months I spent trying to get pregnant, hoping for a miracle, my child, like hers, was a gift from God. In receiving that gift, in offering my body as a recipient of life-giving power, I, like Mary, was never in control. *Let it be, according to your will.* That approach was my part of the bargain: I was a vessel of new life, but that life was never truly mine. The course of that child's life and death were—for me as for Mary—out of my hands. At the altar next to the wellspring, I lit a candle for Phil, and I said a prayer, hoping for nothing more than emptiness.

As we left the church, David approached me. He took both my hands in his, looked into my eyes. "Mary's son's death was for her an experience of the resurrection: that from death can come new life, opportunities and revelations never dreamed of before. So can it be for you."

One morning, we gathered to celebrate the Eucharist at the Church of the Primation on the shore of the Sea of Galilee, reputed to be the place where the disciples were fishing all night without success. Our reading from the Gospels was the story of what happened then. Just after daybreak, Jesus appeared to them, though they did not know that it was he. "Cast the net to the right side of the boat, and you will find some," he said. They did so, and they hauled in so many fish they did not know what to do.

In David's homily, he shed new light on the story for me. This story is not about fishing off the side of the boat that is the opposite of left, he said. It is about casting your net in the right place—where the fish are. As I sat there, looking out over the gray waters, I suddenly heard him. In life, that lesson means not to struggle, to push, resist, or try to control. It means to receive, to accept, to yield, to go with the flow. For me, I could suddenly see that wishing I had my son back was like fishing off the wrong side of the boat. No fish are there; Phil is gone. That is done. I need to pull in my nets and cast them elsewhere, in a place where there is something to be caught. Then, promises the Scripture, I will discover bounty beyond my wildest dreams.

We ended the trip in Jerusalem. On one of the last afternoons we walked the Via Dolorosa, the Stations of the Cross, the last journey Jesus took before he was crucified. Each step taken by this other son condemned to death took hold in my imagination. I saw him carrying the unbearable weight; felt him stumble; heard him as he stopped, saw his mother, and said, "Woman, behold, your son." I became that mother, my son became that son, and I lived death all over again in that dusty Jerusalem street. I wept, though he said, "Don't weep for me," and I envied Mary receiving her son's broken body in her arms.

Any death, David reminded us later at the site of the Garden

Tomb—important as it is—reminds us of the sanctity of life. Jesus' resurrection is about his transformation from living a time-and-space life to being a spiritual presence. For us, Jesus' "coming again" is a symbol of our own transformation, something we wait for in our lives, our own rebirth to a new way of seeing, a new way of living. The Way, the path of a Christian, is a daily conversion, a movement toward wholeness, toward openness. Life is to be treasured—even in the face of death—and embraced as sacred.

The trip to Israel was one kind of pilgrimage, a journey of the spirit. But I had another barrier to face in coming to terms with Phil's death: physical risk and how it might play out in my own life. Six months later, Angus and I embarked on an Outward Bound expedition to New Zealand. Eight of us, all friends already, went with two guides. We trained heavily for the trip to prepare for the forty-pound packs we would carry on our backs. I had imagined that our hike in New Zealand would be through rolling green sheep meadows, but in fact we trekked in Mt. Tongariro National Park, a desolate, treeless, rocky landscape on the North Island at the foot of three volcanoes.

The first afternoon, after hiking for four hours or so, just as we were nearing the place we were to camp for the night, the rain begun. At first it was a fine, gentle mist, but as we hiked, the rain and cold intensified. Soon came a blinding, torrential downpour, pelting our faces and backs, soaking and freezing our clothes, boots, and packs. We had no tents with us, only open plastic tarps, as this Outward Bound experience was intended to challenge.

We huddled under the open tarps, scraping together a half-cooked dinner of dried pasta mix. We were cold. We lay in wet sleeping bags shivering all night while the rain poured down, running in streams over our plastic ground cloths, puddling under our frozen feet. As we huddled together to keep warm, I tried to pretend that I was Phil. I knew that he would be upbeat, probably delivering hilarious one-liners, even in these circumstances. I was not upbeat. I was tired and cold. I was afraid—afraid of freezing, even afraid of dying. As I lay there in a half-sleep, I could feel him near, see his smile, hear his words of encouragement.

The rain continued as morning finally diluted the darkness. We broke camp and hiked in wet gear until at last the sun came out. We stopped and laid our clothes and sleeping bags out on bushes to dry in the warm breeze. I pulled Phil's crazy purple mirrored sunglasses, which I had brought along on the trip, out of my pack and put them on. As the magnificent landscape around me glowed with new light, I knew Phil was patting me on the back. "Good work, Mom. Now move!" We picked up our walking sticks, donned our heavy packs, and began a slow trek toward the volcano looming in the distance.

The third night of the trip, we camped near a stream at the foot of a steep ridge, leading straight up to a cluster of steam vents bubbling up from some underground source. We laid our sleeping bags out under the stars. The night was cold. I knew that in the morning we would have to climb the rocky cliff that loomed above us, and I slept fitfully.

In the morning we loaded up our heavy packs to begin the ascent up the ridge. My stomach was knotted, my teeth even chattered in the chill of dawn. As I climbed, as we rose one hundred, then two hundred, then three hundred feet in the air, my thoughts shifted again to Phil. I thought about him climbing his last mountain, burdened with his own heavy pack, loaded with warm clothes and a sleeping bag for the injured climber. My own load pressed down; the pack creaked. My shoulders ached. My boots were unstable, dislodging stones as I negotiated the steep, rocky trail in the big gusts of wind. I began to be discouraged, weighed down by grief. Tears welled up, blurring my vision. We had climbed almost a thousand feet already, and certain death was straight down to my right, just off the narrow, slippery path. I looked down, terrified. My stomach turned inside out. This is how he died, I thought, falling as if from here, losing his balance and careening down a drop-off like this one. I began to panic. I was paralyzed. I could not go on. I threw my arms around the next big boulder and clung for dear life.

My friends came to the rescue. I felt arms around me, hands patting me. One by one, they took off their own heavy packs, made their way to me along the narrow, treacherous path. "You can do it, Margaret," they said. "It's going to be OK." "You've done a great job so far. Phil would be so proud of you." Gradually I stopped trembling. Slowly I stood up. They helped me to shoulder the cumbersome pack once again. I anchored my gaze to the path in front of me and—one step at a time—continued slowly all the way to the top. Finally I was there! The view was spectacular, exhilarating. I could feel something like the euphoria Phil must have experienced in reaching a mountain summit. I felt so alive, sure that Phil chose this life he led. I knew that even if somehow I had been able to keep him from climbing, to shield him from risk, that he would in some sense already have been dead.

For Christmas his last year, Phil had given friends and family members each some Nepalese prayer flags, five squares of rough cotton fabric strung together: a blue one, a white, a red, a green, and a yellow, all imprinted with Sanskrit prayers, surrounding the image of a god or perhaps the Buddha. He told us then that he loved the decorative flags for their color, mounting his own string on the wall of his room. Shortly before I left for New Zealand, I had called Nicole and asked her about the significance of the prayer flags. She told me they're to be flown at the tops of mountains to free the spirit of the dead. The blue flag was supposed to point east.

Now, at the summit, I pulled the prayer flags out of my jacket. The wind whipped, snapping the cloth as we checked the compass and anchored the blue one to the east. One of our friends said a prayer of thanksgiving for Phil's life, and we sat in silence, watching the wind catch the colors in the morning light, feeling Phil's spirit take flight out over the breathtaking wilderness below. Then we stood up to retrace our steps back down the mountain.

CHAPTER 25

Sacred Space

The soul prospers in an environment that is
concrete, particular, and vernacular. It feeds
on the details of life, on its variety, its quirks, and its
idiosyncrasies.

Thomas Moore

For more than two years after Phil's death, his room remained just as
he had left it. The posters stared down from the walls; the bulletin
board items faded and gathered dust. On the bottom shelf of the
bookcase, right next to the door as I passed by, sat two favorite pairs
of stuffed animal slippers—white bears and pink pigs—worn and
ragged from use and matted from Tia dragging them out to chew on
them with regularity.

The room made me sad, every time. On the one hand, it was a
reminder of Phil that I treasured. Having his room still there, still his,
was in a way like keeping him alive, a kind of evidence that I had had
a son. This room was unmistakable proof that having a son had not all
been a dream. On the other hand, the room was dragging me down.
Often I drove home with my mind thankfully on something other
than grief—a pleasant lunch with a friend, a productive, interesting
meeting, a refreshing bout of exercise. I would burst into the house,

my spirits high, then pass the room and come crashing down with a thud.

I knew the time would come when I would have to do something about his room, but I couldn't bear to disturb the scene. I worried that I would forget, that wiping out his space would be like blotting out his memories. But gradually, I realized that the room clearly needed a transformation. The space would always be Phil's room, but it needed a facelift, a new life.

My first concern was how to preserve the memories. My friend Laura, a photographer, had a great idea: take pictures of it! How obvious, I thought. Why didn't I think of that? So I carefully pointed the camera in all four directions and snapped flash pictures of the room just as he had left it. But I am a writer, not a photographer, and what I came up with was to write down everything in the room, item by item, one by one. As I went carefully through all of Phil's drawers, his shelves, listed the things on his walls, I saw that the objects formed a story, that a portrait of a living person emerged from the word collage on the page. In cataloging the items in the room, I took an intimate journey into his life, touching each thing lightly, holding it in my hand. Once I had written each piece down, I found I had claimed it, taken it into my head and heart, and then I was ready to let it go.

On the walls, the things Phil wanted to look at as he lived:

- A poster for the National Outdoor Leadership School—a bright blue background and a snow-covered mountain. Phil had cut out a small photograph of himself in red hiking shorts carrying a huge backpack and pasted it onto the top of the mountain peak.

- A newspaper ad for Nissan Truck, a "hardbody 4 × 4" that is "ready and willing to take whatever you dish out"

- A Minnesota Vikings pennant, draped with an artificial Hawaiian lei
- A cardboard "skating zone" sign, white with a black silhouette of a cross-country skier, obviously stolen from some park
- A full-page WOODSTOCK headline and a photo of two hippies, cut from the *New York Times* on his birthday in 1989
- Rookie of the Year, Blake Nordic ski team, 1989–90
- A string of Nepalese prayer flags
- A bulletin board, above the desk, crammed with these items, among others: A Jack Daniels Old Time label; a photo of Phil's surprise tenth birthday party; another photo of him, tongue sticking out, riding piggyback on some girl; a plastic pin "Volunteer, Courage Center—Phil Otis"; a pornographic key chain called "Happy Man," showing a well-endowed male profile and a female profile about to lower herself on to his lap; a two-page ad for a Trek bike, aluminum 1200, "lightning quick and naturally strong"; newspaper clipping showing Blake boys' soccer final rankings #19, October 1989; a button "US Out of the Persian Gulf, Bring the Troops Home Now"; a metal postcard of the Matterhorn, sent by me; concert ticket stubs for Paul Simon's "Born at the Right Time" tour; ticket stubs for the Twins, 1987 World Series; huge photo of Blake varsity soccer team; a business card for Kathy Kleven from City Look Barbers; a matchbook from Rosa Flamingo's Italian restaurant on Main Street in Bethlehem, New Hampshire

In the desk drawers:

- A cigar box full of letters, photos, and other memorabilia from Elizabeth
- A packet of letters, cards, and photos from Nicole

- A broken Walkman; a broken Seiko watch
- A letter from a girl whose name I can't read. She is sorry their relationship didn't work out, but she thinks he's "one of the kindest and most sensitive people I have ever met."
- A letter from me, written to him during freshman year in college, about how important it is not to be casual about sex, not only for health reasons, but because it is a most intimate act expressing love and commitment
- A valentine from Angus
- A roll of Nepalese prayer flags

In the bedside table:

- Top drawer: a jumble of miscellaneous photographs; his old knotted, torn baby blanket
- Second drawer: bicycle tools of every description

In the bookcase along the west wall:

Stacks of magazines: *Sports Illustrated, Bicycling, Mountain Bike, Climbing, Rock and Ice*

High-school yearbooks filled with autographs

Complete Guide to Bicycle Maintenance and Repair

Up Your SAT Score

How to Drive Your Woman Wild in Bed

The Fiske Guide to Colleges

Modern Rock and Ice Climbing

South to the Pole by Ski

Roughing It

Woodstock: The Summer of Our Lives

Old Yeller

Lad: A Dog

Bury My Heart at Wounded Knee

The Snow Goose

In High Gear: The World of Professional Bike Racing

25 Bicycle Tours in Maine

The Portable Beat Reader

If Beale Street Could Talk

To Kill a Mockingbird

C. S. Lewis and J.R.R. Tolkien novels

NOLS Wilderness Guide

English/French dictionary

Signpost French (A Guide to French Road Signs)

Riding and Racing Techniques

A Whoopee cushion

In the bookcase along the east wall:

Mass-market crime and science fiction novels

Standing by Words

Zen and the Art of Motorcycle Maintenance

Nothing Special: Living Zen

Spells of Enchantment: The Wondrous Fairy Tales of Western Culture

The Heart Rate Monitor Book

Desert Solitaire

Why I Climb: Personal Insights of Top Climbers

Mountain Journeys: Stories of Climbers and Their Climbs

Mountain Flowers of the Cascades and the Olympics

White Noise

The Curse of Lono

Souvenir photo albums from family trips and Beaver Bay weekends with friends

Travel journals from a family trip to Africa and his cross-country bike trip

The room held more, of course: a stereo, framed family photos, old broken calculators and earphones, an empty wallet, a golf ball or two. I went over it all, fingered each item and carefully noted its existence. Then, liberated from the fear of forgetting, I disposed of it all with a vengeance. I was ruthless. I tossed baskets of things into the trash; I gave books to libraries and posters and banners to my nephews; I sent cards and letters back to their original senders, knowing that the fact that Phil had saved them would mean a lot.

Just as I was loading one of the last baskets of trash, the phone rang. I answered it. My heart stopped in disbelief at the timing. A woman from a shelter for abused women and children was calling to see whether I might have some bedroom furniture to donate. I shook my head in wonder as I gave her our address, and before the sun set that night, they arrived to pick up our gift. I couldn't bear to give Phil's beds away, so I moved those into another room and gave the shelter another old set of twins.

As I worked, I began to shape a vision for what Phil's room should become. I wanted it to be a refuge for me, a space of peace and even spiritual depth. I wanted to feel that memories of Phil, his spirit really, could live in there without the room being a shrine. The space would have a whole new identity but clearly still mark the fact that he had lived. I knew it needed to be the place that would sustain my daily practice of meditation, one that I could associate with silence, with tranquility, with openness to the spirit. I wanted his room to be the place where I would go to tune into that pilot light flickering steadily inside of me.

I had had a steady practice of meditation for four years before Phil died. I had continued that morning ritual that grew out of studying hatha yoga (the physical postures) and *pranayama*, the discipline of breathing patterns. Though rooted in the study of Eastern traditions, meditation for me took on a Christian content. David Keller, Thomas Hand, and others had shown me the long tradition in Christianity of silent or contemplative prayer. I had begun to learn meditation by repeating the St. Francis prayer over and over each morning. It was a mantra, or method to keep my mind focused.

> Lord, make me an instrument of thy peace.
> Where there is hatred, let me sow love;
> Where there is injury, pardon;
> Where there is doubt, faith;
> Where there is despair, hope;
> Where there is darkness, light;
> Where there is sadness, joy.
>
> O divine Master, grant that I may not so much seek
> To be consoled as to console,
> To be understood as to understand,
> To be loved, as to love;
> For it is in giving that we receive;
> It is in pardoning that we are pardoned;
> It is in dying to self that we are born to eternal life.

The prayer was long, but its length helped keep me on task, helped me discourage my mind from wandering. Eventually, I shortened the repeated mantra to just a short phrase that David Keller suggested for me. Even though my meditation practice was rooted in Christian contemplative prayer, my years of yoga and fascination with Eastern spiritual traditions had led me to develop a habit of sitting on a cushion on the floor for this daily ritual of silence. I had a large, flat, stuffed, square *zabuton* mat that went directly on the floor, then a smaller *zafu* cushion stuffed with buckwheat hulls that sat on top of it. I was comfortable with this arrangement, and the feel of its soft architecture against my body instantly suggested the quiet and inner focus of my practice. I used a bronze bowl, struck with a wooden, leather-covered mallet that I had found in Japan, to mark the beginning and the end of my periods of silence.

These cushions, which were the heart of the environment I wanted to create, had an Eastern feel to them. I had always admired the spareness, simplicity, and elegance of Japanese design, and I decided then to make Phil's space into a Japanese room. Phil had a Japanese streak himself. At Bates, he signed up to take beginning Japanese. His plan, at the beginning of sophomore year, was to learn Japanese, then spend a semester as part of Bates's program in Kyoto before he graduated. He did not do well in the course, and he eventually abandoned the Kyoto plan. Still, I remembered his enthusiasm, his joyous use of Japanese phrases off and on for the last few years. I knew he would approve of my plan for our room.

I pulled out the carpet, stained with years of boot mud and bicycle grease. Behind the bed, along the edge of the carpet, I even found crusted remains of vomit—a night of high-school debauchery that had apparently never been entirely cleaned. In place of the old wool rug, I laid down sisal carpeting, a natural straw floor covering that felt cool and calm, inviting bare or stocking feet, and smelled of a fresh haystack. The cocoa brown walls were repainted a quiet, restful beige, the color of perfect sand. I took down the heavy curtains that had once closed out late spring evening light for a sleeping toddler and shielded a teenager from the piercing morning rays. I hung accordion rice paper shades in their place that let in a soft, mysterious light. I bought a new queen-sized bed, low to the floor, one we could use for guests or my stepchildren returning with partners in the coming years, and covered it with a quilt I had found, a patchwork pieced together from the fabric of antique Japanese kimonos.

On a visit with Heidi in San Francisco, the two of us tromped around to Japanese antique stores, where I found a two-part antique *tanzu* chest for the east wall and a tall bronze candlestick to place on top of it. I learned of a company in Colorado that made *shoji* screens out of rice paper and delicate wood, and I ordered one for the corner of the room, to mark off the area for meditation. In an old Japanese print shop, I found a stack of simple wood cuts—spare, elegant line drawings on rice paper. I spent a long time going through them, admiring their design, and I chose three to mount together in a vertical frame to hang over the low wooden chests. The bottom print is a simple representation of a branch of a persimmon tree—a twig with two leaves and a ripe fruit—fruit of the earth, a symbol of nature, and of our continuing presence in this world. For the center I chose the snow-covered silhouette of Mount Fuji. Mountains in Japan can be symbols of death: the word for coffin—*yama oke*—translates "mountain box," and a funeral procession begins with the call *Yama Yuki!*: We go to the mountain! For Phil, who died on a mountain, the print is his gateway into the next world. The last print, mounted on top of the other two, shows a swallow soaring free, gracefully skirting a wisp of a willow branch against a clear sky.

Heidi and Andrew were home for Christmas, the third since Phil's death. The day had been a hard one. Just like every Christmas since the first, the weight of the grief descended on me in the weeks before the holiday. The second year, Angus and I had escaped again, flown to my parents' house in Tucson. But this year, the third, we had both decided the time had come to face Christmas at home. We would have to tackle it sooner or later, and now seemed as good a time as any.

On Christmas Eve morning, I had suggested to Angus that we visit the cemetery, but he had thought it was not a good idea, that such an outing would be too sad, that we needed to do our best to keep up our spirits. That thought had depressed me, making me feel that no one cared anymore, that no one wanted to remember Phil. In the kitchen at breakfast, when one of the kids said something to me I no longer remember, something impatient but totally normal, I felt put upon, rejected. I longed for my own son, who I rationalized would never have said anything of the sort. I grabbed three white tulips out of the centerpiece on the table meant for Christmas Eve dinner, ran upstairs, threw on my coat, and with a loud slam of the door jumped in my car and headed for the cemetery.

Almost no snow had fallen yet that year, and the ground was still brown, the slab of granite still visible, carved with Phil's name. I laid the tulips on the gray face of the stone, sat down on the frozen turf, rested my head on my knees, and exploded into wracking sobs that echoed out over the acres of cold stone monuments. I held back not at all, letting self-pity wash over me. In one of my gasps for breath I heard leaves crackling. I was aware that footsteps were approaching, but I didn't care then who heard me. In fact, I held a kind of satisfaction in the horror that I imagined such a picture of grief would present to a total stranger.

I felt a hand on my back, looked up, and saw Todd and his daughter Madeline. Like me, they had stolen away from the Christmas scene in their own kitchen, escaped to this place where Phil's memory ruled, where forgetting was out of the question. I breathed deeply into their presence, felt the comfort of their companionship, and began to relax. We cried together, the three of us, remembering Phil and sharing our loneliness on this hardest of all days. I felt purged, freed of the pressure that had built up inside of me.

Just before we sat down to Christmas Eve dinner, we all four gathered in the new room, finished in a frantic flurry of early December effort. The sun had set, so light was very low. Heidi sounded the bronze gong. Then I read what I had written earlier in the day:

> This is Christmas. It comes during the season of darkness, when nature is asleep and the shadows of our days are long. It is a time when we yearn for the return of the light and the warmth of the sun.
>
> Life too has its seasons: of darkness and of light, of sorrow and joy, of despair and of hope. To be truly alive is to experience all of these, to know in our hearts both laughter and tears.
>
> As we gather in this space that has fond memories for all of us, let us celebrate its transformation, its new life.

As Andrew lit the candle, Angus read, "We light this candle to rededicate this room and to bless its new life. Let its glow bring light, joy, and hope to all who enter here. Let it be a place that is welcoming to those who stay here. Let it be a place for laughter, for silence, and for peace. As the swallow takes flight over the mountain, let it be a place where spirits soar."

Heidi sounded the gong once more, and we went downstairs to begin our Christmas celebration.

CHAPTER 26

No Tomorrow

Time heals not; it extends a sorrow's scope
As goldsmith's gold, which we may wear
like hope.

J. V. Cunningham

"Time will heal," they said over and over. "You will see. *Time will heal.*" Like a mantra the words repeated in my head, came from the mouths of friends, stared up at me from the pages of carefully penned letters. What did that mean? I wondered. Was time—the endless succession of hours and days—like a balm that would soothe the wound, suture it, then fade the scar, erasing it? Was time a road to forgetting, a path that I must follow to a place beyond memory, beyond sadness, beyond mother love?

Phil was the light of my life, my most cherished friend. I did not want him to fade, recede, or dissolve. If, in a moment, the past and future could explode and fall at my feet in a heap of dust, then what was time? And if this child held my whole life, then what would healing mean?

In the second April after Phil's death, I was bent on some errand, walking through the cosmetic aisle of a suburban department store. I was distracted, pressing deliberately through the crowd, looking for an escalator. A familiar voice pierced the public hum: "Hello, Phil's mother!" I stopped in my tracks. I knew the voice right away: Gert, the woman who used to work at our neighborhood grocery store, the one who used to prowl the aisles looking for lost souls to direct to the crackers, the green taco sauce, the pitted olives. She loved Phil. From his first shopping trip at two weeks old, she would find us each time, examine him, respond to him. As he grew, she kept up with us, with him, exclaiming that she couldn't believe he was already three, six, ten . . . could it possibly be, in college? All this took place long after he found his legs and rarely shopped with me anymore.

Now she stood there grinning at me from a cloud of perfume, a basket of samples on her arm, calling to passersby to offer them a sniff of an aggressive new scent. I knew she didn't know that Phil was dead. I had looked for her at the grocery store in the weeks after the accident, but I had learned that she no longer worked there, that she had retired about the time of his death. She must have missed the newspapers, the television stories.

Now I reached out, touched her shoulder, looked into her eyes. "Phil died, Gert," I said. "He was killed a year and a half ago in a mountain climbing accident."

Her eyes suddenly brimmed with tears, filling my own to overflowing, spilling down my cheeks. I saw that for her Phil had just died at exactly that moment. Until then, he had lived blissfully in her memory, the pudgy, smiling baby, the reaching-out blond toddler, the friendly teenager; the Phil that Gert knew had been fully alive until that moment. If I had not run into her, for her, he would be living still.

I saw then that Phil was not one person but thousands. To each individual whose life he touched, he was utterly unique, a composite of experiences and interactions between the two of them. He had died not once, but thousands of times. Looking back on his life, to create or circumscribe a discrete "being," a separate person that moved through the world is impossible. Instead, he was a series of encounters that enhanced two lives in the moments they occurred. What we are to each other is not two bodies existing separately, but our merged, shared experience, a mutual touching in a series of present moments.

The second Halloween after Phil's death, I was in the corner drugstore, and my eye fell on a T-shirt displayed under the glass counter. "Ashes to ashes, dust to dust," it read: "Life is short, so party we must." I smiled to myself. That was you, Phil, I thought. You knew that from the very beginning. And thank God you did.

How differently now I see them, the same moments. I would pass by his room, knowing it was the night before a big test. I could feel the throbbing of a bass keeping rhythm, pulsing through the floorboards. There he would be, strutting about the room, wearing boxer shorts that were generous in size hanging loosely over slim hips, belly button exposed, a suggestion of male hair in a tangle down the center line. He'd be moving, keeping rhythm to the music of his latest CD, living somehow *in* the music, utterly oblivious to me, to the day, to the test that loomed. The music and dance were a form of meditation, I see now, a way of living utterly in the present.

In those days, my stomach would cramp with frustration, my hands forming into a determined fist that longed to grab him, sit him up straight in his chair, and make him be serious about his future. Don't you *care* about getting into a good college? Don't you *see* that a good college will help you get a good job? Don't you *understand* that today matters for tomorrow? I believed utterly in his future, which was my future too. I wanted the best for him, wanted him to lead a fulfilling life and to be able to take advantage of all the opportunities that were offered. Phil, on the other hand, lived as if tomorrow didn't exist.

Well, there *was* no tomorrow. Did he know it? Or did he just know how to live? Phil understood what I have been struggling to learn: that all we really have is this moment. The past dissolves into memory, the future into fantasy, and the present—ever changing, never ending—is, in its elusive nature, the only reality. I see now that, to me, Phil was a succession of moments in which we were present to one another, which is what each person in my life is to me now. Those moments adhere in memory and, over time, come together to build a collective relationship, but the only opportunity we have to be in that relationship is an individual moment that presents itself in the here and now. If we languish in memory or jump ahead obsessing about the future, we miss the life that is happening here, right under our noses. We squander the only real moments we have.

Phil understood how to live in the present, and I know that he would urge me to do the same. He would point out that grief, real as the feelings are, is about holding on to the past. He would urge me to open my eyes and ears and appreciate the world around me now, today. He would remind me that doing things solely because they will lead to some future outcome is giving up the experience of a sure thing: what is going on right under my nose.

So now I work hard on learning to live in the present. I return to yoga class, week after week. Many days I practice a series of postures on my own. I collect myself, gather energy inward, try to bring my thoughts quietly to a halt. Then I assume a posture, whatever it is. Let's say it is a standing pose—*utthita trikonasana*, for example, the extended triangle pose. I stand straight and tall, arms at my sides. Then I jump my legs about three feet apart and raise my arms to shoulder level, holding them straight out, parallel to the floor. I open my right foot to the side, pointing the same direction as my right arm, then turn the toes of my other foot in slightly. Keeping my two feet firm on the floor, I tip my body over, bringing my right arm down perpendicular to the floor and my left arm straight up in the air. I hold my right ankle with the lowered arm. My chest is open, my body faces forward, and I turn my head to look up at the ceiling.

This pose, like so many, looks easy on someone else, but it is complex and difficult. I have to work hard to keep my balance. My feet want to slide apart; my chest wants to cave in, to roll forward and resist opening up and exposing itself as the pose forces the chest to do.

To turn my head and look up is hard on my neck and shoulders. The pose looks solid and firm, like the pyramids of Egypt, the wide base supporting the towering upper arm, but in truth the stance is dynamic, precarious, calling on all my strength to resist the pressure to fold, to fall, to collapse.

As I stand there for a minute or so, all of my thoughts are concentrated in this effort. My attention shifts from one part of my body to the next, fighting the urge to slip, calming a shaking muscle, searching for an anchor, for stability in the pose. No past, no future. I am utterly here and now, riveted to this body, one with this dynamic, physical triangle I have become.

Doing this series of postures is good for my body. They stretch my muscles, creating space in aging, calcifying joints. The exercise builds strength and stamina, helping me understand that I am one unified organism, body, mind, and spirit. But most important, the yoga teaches me how to stay present.

After fourteen or so years of study, I find now that regularly during the day, I come back to myself. I may be lost in feeling, in analysis, in daydream, when suddenly I snap into awareness. I come home from wherever I was in my mind's eye, back into my body. I feel it at once, and my attention fills its own space and does not stray. The possibility of leaving then does not exist; I am rooted in this spot, this day, in this hour, this moment. It is habit, training. I have learned the attitude by working my body, but the study serves to ground and anchor my spirit and to help me not to miss the life that would otherwise pass me up, the life that is happening under my nose while I am somewhere else. Why should I be lost to memories of my son when the sun is shining on me now, when the grass is alive and growing at my feet, and I might miss a flower about to unfold?

In the months and years since Phil's death, I have slowly returned to the practice of meditation as another kind of training in living in the present. The week before Palm Sunday in the third year, Angus and I returned to the House of Prayer for a Meditation Intensive Weekend, led by David Keller. "Leave all you have and come . . ." read the brochure. The weekend would involve a commitment to two whole days of silence. For me it was a chance to deepen my still sporadic practice; for Angus, who wanted more than a casual introduction to meditation, the opportunity was daunting but perfect. Along with loose clothing and my meditation cushion, I packed my journal:

Friday night

We arrived at the familiar stone and wood building nestled in the woods, and settled into our small white cubicle. After a pleasant supper in which we met and chatted with our fellow participants, we had an orientation and completed our first session of sitting meditation. From now on—except for a couple of question-and-answer sessions—we will all be silent until the end of the program on Sunday. Everyone in the group seems to be so nice—some more experienced like me, some totally new to this like Angus. We are all in it together. I am a little afraid. Will my legs be able to take the long sitting times? Will I simply burst with the need to chat? Will my practice deepen in some tangible way?

After breakfast Saturday

An early morning walk in the frigid air, birds singing, frost on the grass, Angus at my side, in silence. We walk to the river. A muskrat paddles along, breaking the mirrored surface of the water with his rhythmic, powerful motions—automatic, like our own breathing in, breathing out.

At breakfast I was reminded of the wonder of silence: what an amazing thing it is to eat together without speaking. The persona begins to fall away, the face to relax into the effortlessness of this existence. How much energy we normally spend trying to charm, to impress, to be witty or cool! This morning we chew slowly, focus on the exquisite tang of a slice of orange, the sweet burst of flavor from a dollop of jam, the crunch of an earthy slice of bread. We listen to soothing chants playing in the background. We are not in a hurry. "No one," intoned David during our early meditation this morning, "can rush a sunrise."

Later, Saturday morning

Between twenty-minute segments of sitting in silence, we do fifteen minutes or so of walking meditation. We rise and walk slowly, one step at a time around the periphery of the room. "As we walk," David says, "remember with each step that it is the only step there is, that each moment is the only moment there is."

During the break, I step outside. The air has warmed since dawn and it feels like spring. I start a slow walk alone along the wooded path behind the House of Prayer. I settle into a calm, deliberate rhythm like the one we held to inside. I find this walk is a gift, unlike many walks. With each step I am utterly present: to the snap of a twig beneath my foot, to the soft brush of breeze on my cheek, to the warmth of sun on my back. I stay there, each moment, each step. As memory or fantasy begins to intrude, I gently push it away. No, thank you. I am just here now. Suddenly the air is alive, vibrating with a high electric twitter. I am surrounded on every side by the flutter of tiny wings, the sound of birds gently landing on the branches overhead, the mossy log just in front of me. A flock of twenty or thirty migrating juncos— clean little birds, elegant in their slate-colored tuxedos—envelop the patch of woods as if to greet me on their way. They have taken my silence, my emptiness, as an invitation.

Saturday afternoon

Our first afternoon meditation—the fourth session of the day!— was torture. I have chosen to sit on a floor cushion, cross-legged, as I do at home. Because of my yoga classes, the position is usually comfortable. But I no sooner heard the first gong than my back began to ache. A sharp pain started up in my right knee, and my other leg went to sleep. . . . I stuck it out, breathed into the discomfort. After the walking segment, it went away. I could settle back into the silence, breathing in and out. Angus, who like most participants has used a chair, has been surprised at how comfortable he has been.

During the meditation, we were distracted by a knock, then another. It kept repeating insistently, intensely. What is this? Here I am listening to God, and I hear—what?—Jesus knocking at last? I listened, fascinated, letting the tapping punctuate my breathing. Later we learned it was a female cardinal, who— seeing her reflection in a window—railed against her phantom rival, claiming her territory. We too battle our false selves, David reminded us. We waste precious energy protecting our image as reflected in the minds of others. We must come back to the simplicity of breathing in, breathing out, just as we are.

Saturday evening

In meditation I am a shape-shifter: now I am the stream, flowing with my ever-changing thoughts, carried along with the flotsam and jetsam. Now I am the bank: unmoving, watching, still.

Angus and I walk before bed under bright stars, holding hands, not talking. This silence does not separate us. It erases barriers, brings us closer together.

Palm Sunday

In this morning's meditation—our last as a group—I am a mountain. My folded legs and hips form a strong base, rooted on the earth. I am immovable. My head reaches to the heavens. I am in the presence of God. My shoulders and arms form the slopes on which life thrives, illuminated by the morning sun streaming through the window. As time passes, the sun slowly moves on, and I fall into shadow.

Thoughts come and go, just as life brings me joy, then pain; revelation, then devastation. I am a mountain, scene of ever-changing seasons, linked inextricably to the Holy One, the immovable unity that is my source, my life.

CHAPTER 27

Letting Go

This is the Hour of Lead –
Remembered, if outlived,
As Freezing persons recollect the Snow –
First – Chill – then Stupor – then the letting go.

Emily Dickinson

I open my eyes on a summer morning just before dawn. I hear echoing in my mind's ear a line from the communion liturgy: ". . . so to eat the flesh of thy dear son . . ." The dream is vivid, still there. My son has fallen off his bicycle and been run over by a car. I rush to the body in the road and see that it has become a porcupine. I sit down, cradling it tenderly in my arms, and, one by one, I pull out the quills with a pair of tweezers. As I remove each one, it turns into a long green bean. . . .

I lie there in the dim light. I think about the dream, playing with its images and message. Surely I am the grieving mother, perhaps even the one on the road who has been knocked flat by an accident. I feel the dream's hunger, a hunger to touch Phil again, to run my hands over his body, to comfort this flesh of mine. I understand, as I let the dream simmer in early morning consciousness, that the quills—the sharp sting of this death—hold the possibility of transformation. Just as Holy Communion allows me to consume the body and blood, to remember both death and Resurrection, so too this tragic accident can be a pivotal passage for me, even a sacrament. By consuming this death, by turning the quills into beans and embracing it fully, I can allow its pain to become a source of nourishment, to feed new growth in the years to come.

I had another Communion dream one October night in the second year, a couple of months after the first one. This time a congregation was assembled in a huge hall, waiting for the liturgy of the Eucharist to begin. I was behind the scenes, searching madly for a costume—a beige sweater and pants, a pillow to make myself round—for it was I who was to become the loaf of bread: me the bread of life. I was to be offered up, to be consumed by others in the communal sacramental act.

During that week my final manuscript for the spiritual memoir was due. I finished up the work on the bibliography and delivered the completed package on time.

A year or so before Phil died, as I was finishing the writing of *Taking Root*, I had envisioned writing a second book, one about him that would record the joys and trials of raising this son of mine. I even had a title. I had always been irritated that the wedding ceremony focused only on the bride's parents' moment of letting go. I imagined publishing the book about the time Phil might get married, and I would call it *Who Gives This Man?* After his death, I knew that the writing had new urgency, that my temporary title had a whole new meaning, and the story a new focus. For months and months I couldn't even think about such a project. Then one spring night, a year and a half after Phil's death and five months after turning in the manuscript of my first book, I woke in the night filled with energy from a dream.

In the dream I had claimed a special retreat space in which to write. Hanging in the room was what appeared to be a work of art, a textured assemblage, though it was turned with its face to the wall. I flipped it over and noticed its multifaceted surface was polished, more deliberate and shinier on this side. Hanging from the bottom were metal letters that spelled out RAYMOND, Andrew's pet name for Phil.

That spring, I began writing this book, setting aside time each week dedicated to the process. I joined a writing group to sharpen my commitment, to provide a forum for reaction, and to have objective, separate eyes and ears who could monitor my progress. To relive the feelings day by day, month by month, has been hard, intensely painful at times. But I am inspired by Nancy's surgical incision, the importance of keeping a wound like this open, letting it heal slowly from the bottom up and not letting it knit over prematurely on the surface.

As the date of *Taking Root's* publication drew near, my anxiety increased. *Why had I done this?* I wondered. What had possessed me to want to let the world inside my head and heart, to submit the details of a personal conversion to the public for examination and judgment? I was afraid—afraid of mockery, of criticism, of exposure. I thought I might feel as if I were walking around naked while the rest of the world was still dressed.

But the book could not be stopped. Publication came. Agony did not follow. Instead, the experience has been quiet, personal, and moving. A friend wrote that the book had encouraged her to slow down and to find structured time for quiet. A complete stranger in Oregon wrote that the book had inspired her to go forward in a new business she had envisioned. Another—a Catholic who had pushed her childhood religion out of her life—confided that the book had moved her to take a fresh look through adult eyes. Where I had expected harsh exposure, even criticism, I have found connection, intimacy, community. Publication of *Taking Root* has encouraged me to persevere in this second writing project, and—more importantly—it has made me feel alive, as if I have something tangible to give and to leave behind.

The sacrament of Communion is interpreted as a sacrifice, a ritual offering of bread and wine to make present Christ's death upon the cross, God's deliberate sacrifice of his only son. I had just finished reading—the day before I had the Communion dream about the body on the road—a passage in James Michener's *The Source*, which told of a family living about 3500 B.C.E., required by custom to sacrifice their firstborn son. In this agonizing scene, the parents had to take their innocent nine-month-old son, hand him over and watch him be thrown into the ritual fires. To preserve the dignity of the ritual, they were not to cry out in pain. The scene resonated within me. Perhaps the dream was an attempt to turn my own sacrifice into a sacrament of unity and healing. I remembered Kierkegaard's meditations in *Fear and Trembling* upon the story of Abraham, and I thought about it for myself:

> God said to Abraham, *Take your son, your only son Isaac, whom you love, and go to the land of Moriah, and offer him there as a burnt offering on one of the mountains that I shall show you.* (Gen. 22:2)
>
> Abraham, this aged father, bravely bore his only son up the mountain. He lay him down and tied him to a rock, built a fire of sacrifice, and drew a knife to kill him. At the last minute a ram miraculously appeared, a ram for him to sacrifice instead. Isaac was returned to his father unharmed. The lesson has reverberated down through the centuries: have faith: letting go works.
>
> We are told there is something infinitely powerful in the act of opening our grasp, in throwing up our hands. We are taught that the hollow feeling at the pit of our stomach that means we have taken the leap is one we should trust. We are told to give it up, whatever it is, let go of the outcome. We hold our breath, and it is in that moment of suspension—when it is required that we don't know how it will turn out—that faith resides.

One Christmas, when Todd and I were struggling to hold on to our marriage, when I still thought I could win by clamping down, the time came to trim the tree. It was Phil's first Christmas, and I had a particular vision of how it should all unfold. The bare green spruce was set up in the living room. Dusk was falling, and I had carefully laid our strings of lights out along the floor. I looked around for my husband, whose role I thought was to hang them on the tree. He had gone upstairs to our room and fallen asleep on the bed. Perhaps he was tired; perhaps he needed to escape. I was outraged. I shook him rudely awake, told him he had promised to hang the lights, that it was time, that Phil's first Christmas depended on it.

He woke up and came down. He even hung the strands of lights on the tree, but he was not there with us. He was angry, resentful, and full of silent rage. No joy resided in the ritual, no spirit in the gathering. By requiring his presence against his will, I had lost him altogether. By holding on tight to love, I had sacrificed it. I saw the lesson eventually, weeks later. I realized that all that remained in my grasp was an empty shell, but it was too late. My husband had left for good.

As Phil grew, I could see early on that he was a kind of Isaac, a vehicle to test me, one devised by a vigilant sort of God. Phil finally learned to walk only when I dared to peel his tight little fist off my index finger and send him stumbling on alone. He could only learn about stairs when we finally removed the folding wooden baby gate and let him suffer a bump or two on the way down.

But over time, the stakes rose. In eighth grade, he begged to go on that bicycle trip across Colorado. At fifteen there was the climbing course, the electric storm, and the vibrating ice axe in his backpack, his hair standing on end; the summer on Mount Baker dangling over one icy crevasse after another. Each time, I agonized, I wept. I wanted to hold on, to keep him safe at home. But I honored the brave, adventurous heart beating inside of him. I trusted in this gift I had been given. I had faith. I let him go, and each time a ram miraculously appeared.

When Phil was offered the job at Mount Rainier, I let go, just as I had so many times before. I let go, but this time Phil did not come back. What am I to make of this? Part of me wants to end the story there, to draw the conclusion that I had been betrayed. Unlike Abraham's, my covenant was broken. I let go; I had faith, but I did not get to keep Isaac.

The story is not over yet. My son is dead, but I am not. I have a choice. I can tie myself to his rock and light the sacrificial fires. Or I can let go, *really* let go this time. I can turn and make my way slowly back down the mountain, the words repeating in my heart: have faith; letting go works. I can take the leap one more time.

A dream, nearly six years after Phil's death: We are living in the mountains. Phil and I are out at a tea room or pastry shop together. He has his bike and wants to ride home alone. "But you don't know the way," I protest. "It is up over a high pass."

"Yes, I do," he counters, insistent.

I try to convince him to stay with me, to put his bike on the car so we can go home together. He pushes against me, refusing to yield. At last, I begin to feel him winning. I recite the route again: up the ridge, right at the fork, straight over the pass. . . . He nods. I am not sure he is listening. He stands, takes the handlebars.

"See you, Mom," he says.

And I let him go.

CHAPTER 28

For the Living

I took the road we stood on at the start together, I
took it all without you as if
in taking it after all I could most
honor you.

Sharon Olds

Stephen Levine wrote in *Who Dies?* that in loss, we lose the thing that mirrors love in ourselves, the object that reminds us of loving, *is* loving. The love itself is not gone. Now I beam my love for Phil like radar, moving through the world, looking for objects that will bounce it back, register on the screen.

I was talking with Nicole on the phone not long after our anniversary trip to Mount Rainier. She was back in Massachusetts by then, having left Seattle to return home to work near her family. I decided to repeat the plea I had made so many times before.

"I want to be your friend, even after you meet somebody new." This time, instead of protests, there was silence at her end of the line.

"I'm seeing someone," she offered tentatively.

I waited a few breaths. I felt a knot beginning to form in my stomach: jealousy, the fierce, protective instinct that wanted to defend my son from this infidelity. The feeling was grief rising, as I remembered he was no longer alive, no longer in need of my loyalty. Another breath, and then another. I was ready. I remembered my love for Nicole, how I wanted happiness and a full life for her. Part of me leaped with joy that she was beginning to move on.

That day began a new stage in our friendship. Angus and I met the man she began to see. They came together to stay with us for a couple of days in Minnesota on a trip west. Nicole threw the Frisbee for Tia, and the four of us celebrated her birthday together. She is engaged to someone else now, living once again in the shadow of Mount Rainier. We have met him too, and I feel good about them both, together.

But still, I look at her lovely, deep brown hair, and I can't help wondering whether her children with Phil would have been blond like him or dark like her. I want to know her children some day, to isolate her particular half, imagine that my grandchildren might have looked something like them. I tell her I want to stay in touch, to love her and her children. She tells me she would feel incomplete any other way.

Phil's other friends and I keep up too. I get emails from Dryw, living in New York City, working on Wall Street, trading bonds. He and his friend Anne came to stay with us in California for a couple of days. On September 11, 2001, Dryw ran down eight-five flights, narrowly escaping death in the World Trade Center attack. Stew spent a year and a half or so in St. Petersburg, Russia working in real estate, enduring a wind chill even worse than Minnesota's, then went on to graduate from business school. Elizabeth is a fourth-grade teacher now, a job Phil would envy. She is married and expecting her first baby. Keeping up with them all helps me track the passage of time. By watching them, I can imagine how Phil might have aged and developed. These encounters are not sad for me, not "reminders" that drag me down. Phil is always with me, every minute, so they are joyful moments that make me feel closer to him. I know he would love my continuing life with his friends, and they are my friends now too.

We try to have my sister's boys over for dinner one at a time, which helps us come to know them each in a special way. We have followed Andrew's search for the right college and cheered Martin on in his active life of sports. We're fascinated watching Henry's several growing collections—of Buddha figures and bonsai trees.

My godson Maxwell and I have become good friends. He was two at his baptism, just days after Phil's birthday the first year. "Maxwell," I said, holding him in my arms after the service, "can we be special friends now that I am your godmother?"

He looked at me warily out of the corner of his eye. "Not yet," he said.

But a month later, I showed up on his birthday with a toy Jeep, just like my car that he had admired so much. We've had regular outings since then, just the two of us. We've visited the Children's Museum and an electric train exhibit in a suburban shopping mall. We've dined at greasy spoons on chicken soup and at McDonald's on French fries. We've taken in a number of movies and two zoos. He's nine now, a redhead with a big grin and a glint in his eye. I am his godmother after all, so each time we're together, I wait for a pause in the chatter.

"What's in your heart these days, Maxwell?" I always ask.

The answers have been hilarious, but one year—just before Christmas—he waited a beat or two. "You," he answered with a shy smile.

The year has a new rhythm now, a syncopation that disturbs the old patterns. Phil's birthday in late May looms larger than it did when he was alive. We celebrate it without him, remembering him with a special lunch, with calls or notes from his friends. As July rolls into August, I can feel the air grow heavy and thick. The days are suspended, long, and my heart feels guarded, waiting for another shoe to drop. The Christian religion has no rituals to mark the anniversary of a death, but we have designed something with a little help from our Jewish friends. The night before August 12, we take a special candle that is designed to burn for twenty-four hours. Angus and I each share a personal memory of Phil as we light the candle. The next day, we might visit the cemetery, have lunch with my parents, maybe take a long walk outdoors, listening to the birds and feeling the sun warm our bodies. As night comes, we read from a couple of Psalms and extinguish the candle for another year.

Epilogue

February 1999 in the Napa Valley: As stepmother of the bride, I was the first of the three mothers to be seated. I held on tight to my stepson Andrew's arm as he escorted me down the aisle. Though my heart was beating wildly with excitement and anxiety, I tried my best to smile back at all the beaming faces lighting our path—so many of our friends who had flown out to California to be with us, clusters of young people whom I did not know, my own sister and parents. I settled gratefully into my chair in the front row to wait.

As I sat there, as Caley's mother, then Heidi's, were seated as well, I looked around me at this extraordinary and unexpected setting. We had had a vision for this wedding. Heidi and I had been working together for months, talking daily over the details, carefully imagining this moment, thinking of everything we could do to make it perfect. The service was planned outdoors, even though we were in the middle of February, and was going to take place in our new graveled driveway, surrounded by a low, curved stone wall. The designated "altar" was an opening under the arching branches of two old olive trees that framed a spectacular view south down the valley. We would look out over a patchwork quilt of blossoming trees and fields of brilliant yellow mustard, glowing in the afternoon sun. The chairs were to be carefully arranged in rows with mossy pots of white tulips at the ends. The aisle down the middle would be carpeted with a natural sisal runner, strewn with olive and bay leaves and sprigs of rosemary.

But the plans were not to be. We woke that morning in an impenetrable mist. About ten o'clock it began to rain. As I served lunch to Heidi and her bridesmaids, we realized we would have to make do with the tent that had been hurriedly erected over the back terrace the day before. The rain had now been falling for over six hours, pelting the tent, sheeting down the plastic sides, forming into rivulets that flowed inexorably down the slight pitch of the terrace tiles.

We had done our best with a squeegee, blasted heaters into the space, and laid the sisal mat across the tiles to a plywood platform. We massed the pots of tulips at the front to hide the rough edge of its carpeted cover. Now I was shivering in chiffon as warm gusts from the heaters alternated with the wet chill of a misty cloud that blew periodically through the tent.

I reflected, sitting here, that life had intervened in our plans, just like the weather. One couple, two of our very best friends, had had to stay home. His immune system weakened by chemotherapy, he had contracted viral pneumonia and was too sick to travel. Though another good friend had lost her mother five days earlier, here she was anyway, shaken with grief and exhaustion. As I watched Heidi's friends, beautiful bridesmaids, file one by one down the aisle, I knew that one, the mother of a two-year-old, was desperately trying to keep her mind off the biopsy she would have to endure on Monday for a lump under her arm. Another, who missed the rehearsal dinner, had shown up for the wedding despite her father-in-law's death on the operating table the previous morning. *Life takes our carefully constructed visions and vaporizes them, reminding us decisively that we are not in control.*

The music paused. Then the strings began again in new, important strains. We rose to our feet. I looked back toward the house and saw Angus, walking tall through the crowd and beaming with pride. On his arm was his daughter, my own precious stepdaughter, gorgeous in an ivory satin dress, her blond hair drawn back into a low bun, tucked with blossoms of stephanotis, her smiling face radiant. I stole a glance at Caley, waiting on the makeshift altar, and I saw in his spreading grin, his twinkling eye, so much love I thought my own heart would explode.

You are missing this, Phil, I thought. *You would have loved the adventure of this wedding: the rain, the mystical cloud, this crazy tent. You would have been so proud of Heidi and excited to have Caley as a new brother.* But then I stopped myself. *No, Phil, I know better. You wouldn't want me to miss this. I need to pay attention, to be here, every minute—for you too.*

We still live in Minnesota, but we spend almost half the year now in the Napa Valley at the new house where the wedding ceremony took place, a modern house of thick stucco walls, built to last and painted the color of earth, of blood, of rich cabernet. A bubbling fountain spills over a ledge and provides a backdrop of sound. Steller's jays squabble in the live oaks overhead, and wild turkeys scratch in the red earth between the rows of vines.

The whole project was created after Phil. He never even saw the property. Living there, surrounded by vineyards, we are tied to the land. We relax into the rhythm of the year, watching the grapes bud, then slowly mature. We harvest them in September, and up the road at an old winery we are restoring, we are slowly educating ourselves in the art of making wine.

Behind the house, on the wooded knoll that embraces it, we have carved a meditation path through the forest of live oak, madrone, and bay laurel. Cushioned in wood chips, the path winds its way through groves of trees, pausing to turn at a moss-covered stone, at a deep mahogany limb fallen from a manzanita tree, at the peeling, curling bark of a madrone. Two wooden benches wait, where we often stop to sit and take in the breathtaking views over the vineyards. It reminds me of the path Father Hand created at Mercy Center, and like that one, like the road through our neighborhood in Minneapolis, walking it anchors each day, a physical mantra to help keep us in the present moment.

Staying present is a struggle, though, as it always has been. We look back, cherishing our memories of Phil, wishing he were here to share this new life with us. But mostly we look forward—anticipating next year's vintage, hoping for another wedding, counting the days until we see our new granddaughter again, she who was born just as the mustard bloomed last year.